1

TABLE OF CONTENTS

ACKNOWLEDGEMENTS

As my eyes opened on the last day before publishing this book, I was overwhelmed with gratitude. Words could never capture nor describe the joy my heart harbors, as a result of the people around me.

To my Mama:

You are strength in the flesh. You considered us before you considered yourself. You were a slave to what you believed to be right! When you would get frustrated with me, you would force me to sit down and read Bible verses. I know you probably wondered if it was working; but I am the fruit of the investment you made in me all those years. Because of your commitment to me, I am committed to ensuring the rest of your days will be your best days! You are truly my Super Woman, and I love you forever.

To my Granny:

You are my benchmark for stability! I've literally been attached to you from birth; I even had to leave the hospital to be with you! To say you are special to me would be a massive understatement. You are the matriarch of our family, and I trust that the rest of your days will be your best days! I love you forever; especially since I'm your favorite grandchild!

To Restoration Church of Jesus Christ:

You are not just my church family; you are my family! I can't thank you enough for the effectual prayer you constantly extend to me and my family. You are a part of the body of Christ, you serve the city of Dayton, OH; the region; and our world as a lighthouse of hope. I personally believe that we are one of God's favorite churches! I'm proud to serve you, and humbled by your support. I love you; and you can't do anything about it!

To My Pastor and Spiritual Father, the honorable Bishop Lambert W. Gates:

You have exemplified the embodiment of God's love, towards me. Your consistency has stabilized me. You helped me when I felt helpless. When I was weakened and vulnerable, you invested strength into me. You have handled me with care. You have been firm yet fair. You hold me accountable, while leading out of the wilderness, and into the glory of God's favor. For that, I say, "Thank you".

I could not have accomplished a fraction of the feats I have conquered, without help from my amazing supporting cast. The supporters that I want to mention, specifically, are _The Fatherless Son_ book team.

LaRhonda Carson:
You are one of the most intelligent persons I have ever met. Without the benefit of your brilliance, this project would be dull and bland. You are a gift to everyone you've ever shared oxygen with. I never want to imagine my life or ministry without you. Thank you!

Destini Edmond:
Without fail, you raise the bar and manage my monumental moments. Your value is ever-growing; you enhance everything you touch! You have the spiritual Midas touch, and you make me better. You have carried this project from its infancy to its fruition. You epitomize what it means to be a spiritual daughter. Thank you!

Audrey Preyor:
My favorite blood sister! (My only sister). You have traveled the entire long and winding road of life with me—although I had a six-year head start. We have shared grief, triumph, and now we share these pages. This is not my book: this is our book first, and together we are sharing it with the world. I thank you: this book would literally be illegible without your expertise and attention to detail. You are loyalty incarnate. I have committed my life and strength to loving you, as perfect as your love is towards me. Your children are my children. Carter is my son/nephew. Brooklyn-Marie is my daughter/niece. They're going to make it! You're going to make it! We're going to make it!

THE FATHERLESS SON

Gwendolyn Edmond:

I am so honored to be connected to you - you are a gift to the world! Years ago, when I told you that your gift would take you places beyond where a plane ticket could carry you, I didn't know my book project would be one of those destinations! Your selflessness will be rewarded. The hand of God is upon you and he expresses Himself through your creativity. Never doubt yourself, because I don't! Never underestimate yourself. Your capacity is beyond your ability to comprehend - God will accomplish amazing things through you!

You have transformed my intangible vision into artwork that can be seen and appreciated by the entire world. The skillful, intentional approach you give to your craft is worthy of celebration, but most importantly I thank you for being you.

To my family:

Lawrensa Saucer:

Without question, you are the MOST important person the Lord has allowed me to meet! I am a shell of myself without you. Life wouldn't be worth living, and death would be an upgrade if I had to live without you! You didn't marry a pastor, mentor, community activist, or humanitarian—you married a man. You married *me*. However, with your glory being smeared over every element of me, I have grown to become all of these things—and more. This project—and everything I've ever received credit for—was made possible by being filtered through the conduit of your virtue. Thank you for sharing me with the world. Thank you for making me feel like the only man in the world. THANK YOU, and I love you forever.

Sanaa:

My oldest and my beloved first-born...when you were born, you changed my life for the better, forever! I had never seen a baby as beautiful as you before that day. The moment I looked at you, the tears began to flow without restraint—because you were everything perfect about me. You are a trendsetter and you have an anointing for business. You are smart, you are beautiful, you are a leader, you are everything to me. You are from God, and I love you forever!

Alaya:

My clone, my beloved second-born. Of all my children you are the most like me. You are so strong, and a natural protector. Like Sanaa, when I first looked at you, I cried like a baby. I cried because you were so radiant. When you smile, you warm up my life like the sun warms the Caribbean. You are special, the mark of success is on you, and you will win—because you're a winner! You are not like anybody else, so always be yourself. Because after all, YOU are perfect, just the way God made you! You are smart, you are beautiful, you are a leader, and you are everything to me. You are from God, and I love you, forever!

Azaria:

My baby girl, my beloved cuddle bug. You are the most sensitive of us all. Your heart is bigger than your whole body. Just like Sanaa and Alaya; when I first saw you, I cried like a baby. Your beauty and infectious smile was made for modeling. The Hand of God is on you, and favor will follow you all the days of your life! You are the one child that loves to cuddle, just like me! You have my permission to sneak into my room, snuggle next to me, and watch Animal Planet—whenever you want! You are smart, you are beautiful, you are a leader. You are everything to me—you are from God, and I love you, forever!

THE FATHERLESS SON

A Letter to My Son:

Steve Jr. (Junny). I always dreamed of the day that I would meet you. I envisioned you for decades, before I ever got to see you. I studied your countenance in my dreams, and imagined your mannerisms. All of these years preparing to meet you couldn't prepare me for the emotions I experienced when I first laid eyes on you. Your mother and I went through so many difficulties prior to your conception. We were led to believe that more children would never be possible for us. You are truly my miracle baby! When challenging times come, I want you to remember that you are predestined for greatness! When you arrived, I stared at you for hours, just like I stare at you now. My heart is made happy when I remind myself that you are the manifestation of the best version of me; in flesh and blood. You look like me, but much more handsome! You're sharp like me, but much more intelligent! You're everything that I am, and you're everything good that I'm not! Stand on my shoulders; because I want you to see farther than I ever could. Take my baton, and pick up where I left off; so you don't have to start from scratch. I will support you. I will guide you. I will teach you. I will protect you. I will show you how to love your wife by how I love your mother. Most of all, I will love you forever.

In love,
Dad.

THE FATHERLESS SON

A story of rejection and redemption.
What destroyed so many, developed me.

PREFACE

This book is an expression of my heart. Going into this project, I had no idea that it would be so emotionally draining. When I shared (with the very few people I trusted enough to tell) about this book, questions arose concerning this project that I struggled to answer plainly. Was it a biography? Was it a tell-all? Was it an instructional manual?

When I began to think about my earliest family memories, my grandmother's southern cooking was one of the fondest. She would always make gumbo - a mixture of diverse ingredients: shrimp, pork sausage, chicken, a multitude of vegetables, rice, and every other creative yet intentional ingredient she could afford, all simmering in a delicious, flavorful stew. I suddenly thought, "This is that!" This book is my story, but it's not entirely unique to me. It's not a tell-all; but I will tell all that's necessary to ensure that deliverance and the restorative process manifests. At the same time, it will lack the spirit of indictment usually associated with those types of projects. It's definitely an instructional manual, and while I have mastery on the subject of fatherlessness, it is not a do-what-I-say-or-else kind of project, either. In its purest form, it is an expression of my pain, exposure to my process, and acknowledgment of my purpose; with the intent to empower others!

I have failed in so many things, but I've succeeded in so many more. Although I began with a story of rejection, with this book I am also able to acknowledge my redemption. I've heard it said that there are three sides to every story: my side, the other side and the truth. Hopefully, as you peruse the pages of this book, you are not only introduced to my truth or the other truth, but that THE truth about fatherlessness is revealed. As much as I would love to, I could never separate my success, failure and aspirations from my story of fatherlessness. Fatherlessness is a plague that has negatively affected more people than the world could ever know.

This book speaks to my unique story, but fatherlessness itself is extremely common. The world my friends and I grew up in tried to paint the picture that a man who shows emotion is weak. It trained us to believe, even if subconsciously, that any form of dependency is a negative. It trained us to believe that men are men because of their ability to manipulate and abuse women: that a man is a man when he learns how to have his way in every situation, regardless of the implications to others. We were taught to believe that arrogant selfishness is a sign of strength, because men couldn't care less about what doesn't directly affect them.

I know some would argue that this is a completely false and an exaggerated statement concerning what fatherhood is, and I agree that this is a complete misrepresentation of fatherhood. Unfortunately, this is what I grew to believe. I can say this is false today because now I see the world through the eyes of a God-fearing man and an active father. My life has taught me that fatherhood is defined by the individual; it's not the same for everybody. Those previous ideas—what the world taught us fatherhood is—are conclusions that young, underdeveloped minds come to, when they attempt to teach themselves a subject that requires group participation. This book is designed to describe the world through the eyes of one who survived a fatherless existence. I don't use the word "survive" without understanding the gravity that the word suggests. I truly believe that fatherlessness is an intangible war that young boys and girls attempt to not only navigate, but survive every day all around the world.

As I consider my upbringing and how I felt in my small world that seemed so large, it brings to mind the ants in an ant farm. The controlled environment of an ant farm is not the natural habitat for any ant, so if the ant doesn't know how to properly respond to the foreign environment it's been placed in we ought not to judge it too harshly. The ant never asked for the ant farm, it was a life someone else created for them. They are essentially victims of the decisions of another!

The ant in the ant farm lives in a small world compared to the vastness of the world that surrounds it. However, to the ant, there is no world outside of the tunnels and sand pits it navigates everyday. There is no reality beyond the perspective its environment creates. In my youth, I was that ant. The one difference between me and the ant was that the ant had a support system with an unquestioned hierarchy that provided its identity and I had none.

From the very beginning, writing this book pulled on strings of my heart that have not been played since very early in my life. It began to push tears out of my eyes that I could not explain. In most cases we know why we're crying - maybe we're sad, joyful, overwhelmed with pride or simply overly enjoying a moment. Writing this book took me to a place of inexplicable tears, especially since I believed that I had completely healed. At times I cried because I remembered how sad I once was. Sometimes I cried because I was so grateful that I made it out, despite the difficult circumstances that I was forced to endure. Other times, I cried thinking about the rejection I experienced at the hands of some of the people I loved. For whatever reasons, the tears came.

I believe this book was more for me than for anybody else. I'm excited because I believe that the portion of my life - that for so long has been a source of pain for me - will one day be a source of deliverance for others. This is no ordinary book. It isn't an autobiography. This isn't just my story, this is *the* story. The story of fatherlessness.

I pray that everywhere this book goes, the hearts of absentee fathers are pricked. I pray that they gain the strength to redeem lost time with their children and families, that they seek forgiveness and are able to forgive themselves. That they won't allow pride to win; that they will go beyond all of the lost time they can't get back, and maximize the time they have remaining. My prayer is that they become one with the divine purpose of fatherhood, and begin to walk in the shoes that were fashioned for them.

My prayer is that this book ministers to single mothers struggling to endure the strain that comes with attempting to fill a role they weren't built to fill. I pray that their hearts - broken not for themselves, but for the brokenness in their children - will one day be mended; because deliverance and restoration are at the door.

My prayer is that every daughter who became vulnerable to the wrong man, because she didn't have the presence of the right man, will be healed. For every time she questions her own value, her own worth, and her own importance in this rugged and cruel world, that this book speaks to her; informing her of the value that's been placed in her, and preserved for a time like this. That she won't give up and give in to the pressures of a society that attempts to make her feel like independence alone is the goal. Although it's good to be independent, we learn independence from consistent dependence on the right sources.

My prayer is that every son will come to know himself and never question if his existence is a mistake. That he turns around and no longer runs toward a swift destruction because he's embraced a spirit of rebellion, attempting to soothe the pain of rejection. My prayer is that every son embodies every quality he wishes was exemplified in his life, that he so desperately needed Also, that he doesn't die an underdeveloped boy, but that he grows into a fully mature and responsible man. I pray that this book will help him become the man and the father he wished for.

Lastly, my prayer is extended to the children who were fatherless while their father resided in the home. Those abused - mentally, physically, emotionally, sexually or spiritually - by the one man they should have been able to trust. It's my prayer that the ministry of restoration manifests through every sentence, and that the restorative power of deliverance overwhelms every reader and that the eternal glory of God's perfect provision comforts every heart and soul. My prayer is that every reader no longer identifies with the pain of being a fatherless son!

THE FATHERLESS SON

PART ONE

WHAT IS FATHERHOOD?

CHAPTER 1:

THROUGH THE EYES OF A FATHERLESS SON

I remember the very first time I realized that I was fatherless. I must have been about nine or ten years old and it was the day I met my best friend's father. It was sunny outside and it had already been a great day of fun and laughter! We ran through our neighborhood freely, without a care in the world. We pulled ponytails and ran away laughing, torturing every girl we could catch. Most of all we sat under the last standing shelter at our neighborhood park and talked about our future.

Somehow, we developed the crazy idea that we would become rap stars, and change the world through our newly acquired riches. Our families would be shipped off to Hollywood to live the rest of their days in matching mansions, in a neighborhood surrounded by one huge fence! I distinctly remember thinking and feeling like the day just kept getting better! It's important to note that my tight group of best friends and I didn't consider each other as friends only. To this day, we are *family*. This particular friend and I always considered ourselves to be brothers, and we might have had the closest bond that two non-blood related people could ever have.

The moment I met his father, I said to myself, "Since he's my brother's father he's going to be my father, also." I affectionately called him "pops" from that day forward. We went on with our carefree lives, until something happened that forever changed me; mentally. Roughly two years later, I was in my backyard with my mother. (I'm sure my mother had me working against my will!) My friend and his father came walking up the alley, and we introduced our parents. At that moment, I was struck with the reality that my mother and his father had never met each other. When these two strangers met, it sent a very real tremor down my spine, and a dark, depressing reminder came to mind, "You don't know your father." At that moment, I came to the realization that regardless of who I *called* my father, the truth was I *had* no father.

I grew up really poor. I assumed that we lived an average life that would be considered middle class. I didn't realize how deprived we were until years later when I left home and learned that not everybody grew up like I did. My mother was successful at maintaining a sense of stability for my little sister and I. She provided a stable roof over our heads, the evidence being that I only lived in two places my entire childhood. No matter what we lacked within those walls, we always had shelter. Some people may consider that to be commonplace, but many of my family and friends don't have that testimony.

THE FATHERLESS SON

Our first home was in Arlington Courts, "the projects", on the west side of Dayton, Ohio. Eventually, we were able to move into a small, two bedroom home on Stewart Street, not far from Arlington Courts. Although that move in my mind represented advancement—we were "moving on up" just like The Jeffersons! - my sister and I weren't able to experience many of the luxuries that other people regularly enjoyed. I thought things like vacations, nice cars parked in the garage, floor model TVs that actually worked, family game night and going school shopping (to pick out clothes that we actually wanted) were just fantasies on TV! My perspective was so skewed that I thought people who had an upstairs in their house and more than one car were rich. Regardless, my sister and I were happy and surrounded by friends and family that loved us!

The horrible, unintended consequence from my mother being such an effective provider is that I never really got to know her like I wanted to. She was always working, and when she was home she was usually sleeping, getting ready to go to work the next job. Although my mother consistently held two, sometimes three jobs at a time, many times she still visibly struggled to hold things together. However, in spite of all of that, she never complained. She was such an inspiration!

I always blamed the father that I didn't know for making the mother, who I did know, have to work so hard; as he failed to provide any relief. Everything that I perceived to be wrong, harsh or unfair, I believed he could have saved us from. At times, I wondered if he was somewhere close; watching my mother go to work, come home, sleep a couple of hours, then get up and go back to work. I wondered was he somewhere close, when our lights were turned off and we had to learn to live in the dark with candles and flashlights. Sometimes, I wondered if he was nearby when I would be rebellious - refusing to cut the grass. I knew my mother lacked the energy to yell at me about it and as a result the grass would be almost my height before I ever got around to cutting it. I thought angrily, "*I wish he would come tell me to cut the grass*, this is supposed to be his job anyway!"

I always wondered was he somewhere close, watching us as we got on bus after bus after bus with our arms full of groceries, struggling to keep it all together? Was he driving past us, enjoying his life, while we were left to fend for ourselves? I always wondered when we didn't have food and were hungry, did he have enough money to pay for food but just refused to do it? I wondered if he was dead and if so at what age did he die? I wondered if somebody had killed him, maybe because he was such a bad person. Then I got angry because sometimes I didn't care, and sometimes I did. I got angry when I cared, because who in their right mind would care about a person that couldn't care less about them? And then sometimes I got angry because I didn't care, and I wondered who in their right mind wouldn't care about their own father being dead?

Asking myself those questions and lacking legitimate

answers caused me to develop a hatred for a man that I didn't even know. I then began to develop my own perception of what being a father really was. As you may imagine, it was hard for me to develop a true picture of what fatherhood looked like because most everyone I was closely connected to was essentially fatherless.

Most of my friends and family suffered from the same fatherlessness that I did, just in different forms. Some of them had fathers who were inconsistently present, here today and gone tomorrow, but from my perspective at least they impacted their children's lives. Some of them had fathers who never came around, but at least they knew who their fathers were and they saw them once in a blue moon. Some, and I still considered them lucky, as perverted as it may sound, had fathers in the home, but they were abusive fathers who created a dysfunctional environment. For others like myself, there was no sign of our father anywhere in sight. It's also true that there were individuals who actually had active fathers in the home. They had fathers who were present, good examples, and responsible men; but those situations were few and far between.

The first example of a father figure that I can remember was my grandfather. Oh, how I loved my grandfather; and I know he loved all of his grandchildren, too. I remember hanging under him real close. Whether he was showing us the way, or not paying us any attention - I'm not completely sure which he did most often - he was there. Unfortunately, my grandfather was a chain-smoking alcoholic, with his own set of issues that negatively affected his family.

Still, I loved my grandfather and (as a naive grandson) I have only positive memories of him. My grandfather died when I was in the eighth grade, and I didn't know how to deal with the loss. It was a loss I don't think I ever fully processed. Even at that young age, I was consumed with considering what the rest of the family was going through. I don't even remember crying. I still think about him, and wonder how I might have turned out if he were still alive.

My internal tears flow when I see pictures of the two of us. Unanswered questions weigh heavily on me. What would he think of the man I've become? What would he say about "the pastor", "the leader", "the father"? Would he approve?

Two other positive examples of fatherhood in my life were two of my uncles. They were not my blood uncles, but were related by marriage, and I couldn't love them any more if we did share the same blood. I remember as a kid, noticing my older uncle, who was - from my vantage point - a very involved father; actively mentoring all of his nieces and nephews.

My earliest memories of hanging out with him and all of my cousins are hilarious, even now! I was certain he and his family were rich, because they had a car and an upstairs in their home! I vaguely recall him piling many of us up in the back seat of his car (breaking, I'm sure, multiple traffic safety laws). He was short in stature, like me, but he quietly gave me confidence because he was an obvious leader. He was an example of strength. He would lift heavy weights, and it looked effortless. I wanted to be like him when I grew up! I remember thinking how lucky my cousins were because they got to go home with their dad. My grandfather and uncles made a positive fatherly impact on me, but none of those men were my father.

Unfortunately for me, the negative examples were far more abundant and, often times, right before my face. Those were the images I had to go home with every night. Although those three men were present as far back as I can remember, the lack of a father in my home pushed me to pay more attention to family structures that looked like mine.

My experiences begin to shape what fatherhood was in my eyes...selfish. I began to think being a man meant taking care of self first or self only! The men that I was close to outside of those positive examples, exhibited an arrogant selfishness. I often wondered how a man could be okay, knowing his children might be hungry right now and not be motivated to do something about it. I began to self-medicate with unhealthy relationships and destructive behaviors, attempting to access my feelings on my own.

As a child, I obviously did not accurately discern the truth concerning fatherhood. I was conflicted, caught between my growing notion of what fatherhood was and the compassion I felt for people in my shoes. On one hand, I believed fatherlessness was normal. I believed that most fathers lacked compassion because they refused to be inconvenienced for the convenience of their children and family. On the other hand, I questioned my feeling that compassionless living was wrong, and I thought those feelings meant I was being "soft" and I would be mad at myself because I believed my heart was displaying an inherent weakness. I came to believe the word "father" was synonymous with "selfish"!

Men that I thought were cool had several women—usually a different woman for every occasion. Most of them had multiple children by multiple women and I hardly ever remember seeing them spend time with their children publicly. This added to the shift in my ideology. I began to believe my situation was normal and subsequently the pursuit of multiple girlfriends began to consume me! I attempted to suppress what I considered an unnatural desire to be fathered in exchange for what I believed a man was supposed to look like - a player!

I believed a man's value was measured by the money and material items he possessed. I believed that a father flowed with the proverbial milk and honey the world had to offer and that not having money was not an option for a real man. The idea was that money was so important to the quality of a man, he must be willing to do whatever, whenever and to whomever to get it! A man without money, cars, clothes and women was essentially not a man at all!

As I grew into a responsible man myself, I grew to realize that my perspective was demonically skewed. I had measured men by the bad examples of men in my life. In hindsight, I've learned that our feelings and perspective can deceive us. It was true, I had developed a full perspective concerning what fatherhood was, but my feelings misled me. I learned that ignorance is not justified by emotional stimulation. In fact, an over-dependence on our emotions is what keeps us trapped by the bars of ignorance! It was true that I believed that my concept of fatherhood was accurate because I felt so strongly about it, but it was also true that I was WRONG!

It was true that I believed that my concept of fatherhood was accurate because I felt so strongly about it, but it was also true that I was WRONG!

CHAPTER 2:

THROUGH THE EYES OF A FATHERED SON

Many years ago, after a long church service, an even longer fellowship among us young preachers ensued, as usual. I, always curious, began to ask questions about everybody's ministerial upbringing. One preacher immediately lit up and couldn't wait to tell the story about his ministerial beginnings. His reply was filled with pride and we were all immediately captivated by his beaming eyes and the glare from his shiny teeth as he smiled from ear to ear, talking about his father! His story was one of glory, favor and opportunity! He graciously credited his father and the legacy he was born into. He talked about all that he learned at the feet of his father and his father's father and even what he learned from their peers. He testified of the great esteem he received and favor he gained from men of honor simply because of the family he was born into. He never suffered from the dreadful plague of obscurity that many of us endured.

He was invited to minister in legendary pulpits because of his pedigree and because he walked in the shadow of great men! It was almost like legacy oozed from his pores, and fortunately for him and anyone who would be exposed to his ministry, he was just getting started! Although the legacy did not diminish the commitment, dedication and attention to spiritual discipline he had to put in on his own (and which I believed he was committed to doing) his background served as a ministerial springboard to excellence. I remember thinking with great anticipation, "One day, my kids will be able to say the same things about me!

I've learned that fathers are driven to provide, and will stop at nothing to accomplish this. There's a perseverance born in the spirit of a real father. He will never quit until the job is done. Fathers have a hunter-gatherer component in them that ignites a fire to accomplish for the benefit of those connected to him. He works long hours (sometimes feeling like there's no end in sight), and doing it with a smile; anticipating that his family will benefit from the fruit of his labor. Fathers get their hands dirty and are never afraid of hard work. The work that fathers do is not for their own benefit. They don't hesitate to work their fingers to the nerves to buy food they might never get to taste, because it's what a good father does. Good fathers are examples of leadership and wish to build legacies. It's been said that, "Society grows great when old men plant trees whose shade they know they shall never sit in." - Anonymous Greek Proverb

I could have never expressed a single sentence in this chapter if not for my former pastor and the role he played in my life previously and in my current role as a father. I distinctly remember studying everything about the man I served under for so many

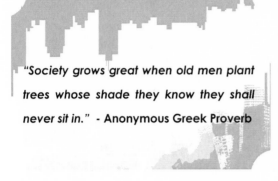

"Society grows great when old men plant trees whose shade they know they shall never sit in." - **Anonymous Greek Proverb**

years, particularly how he dealt with his wife and children. I wanted nothing more in life than to know what fatherhood looked and felt like and this was the first time I saw a man put everybody else before himself. I wanted to be that to my own family one day. I admired how he considered his wife. He was always concerned with her needs and with her safety. It impressed me that he made it his personal responsibility to see that her needs were met and her desires were accounted for. Unfortunately for those who would love to be able to do "just enough", true fathers master the art of going above and beyond. "Just enough" is never enough because there's always more that could be done.

Real fathers take it personally how prepared their children are for life. Sons have to do enough push-ups every night to be strong enough to defend themselves in case a bully is lurking. They are laser-focused on infusing confidence into their children. They initiate games like "see if you can punch my hand" to refine reflexes. Spontaneous and unrestrained wrestling matches break out—just for the fun of it—despite a mother's perspective that none of this is advisable and seems flat out dangerous!

Fathered daughters also have to be comfortable enough to be themselves, not consumed with worry about whether or not somebody will take advantage of them, because in the back of their mind they always know daddy is somewhere watching. As a result, these daughters develop an eye for the guy they should steer clear of! In her mind she'll think something like, "my daddy doesn't talk to me like that" or "my daddy would never act like that"! Because of her inner voice, she is guided towards success! Her smile is free from pain. Life is easier for her and she knows it!

The freedom that comes with being connected to your father makes a child feel as free as a bird. The limitless possibilities go beyond the expression of any verbal language. The beauty of the influence of an active father is revealed in the confidence of his children. The sky seems ever so reachable because nothing is impossible! Nothing limits the creative mind of a confident child. Colors are more vibrant because the world is pure and untainted by the hardship and anguish of feeling vulnerable. Everything that child does has a different energy because after all, there's the assurance that daddy will be right there passing out high fives, ice cream cones and inescapable hugs.

Words could never completely capture the feeling of wonder and bliss the presence of a father provides. A fathered son thinks, and rightfully so, "I don't have to

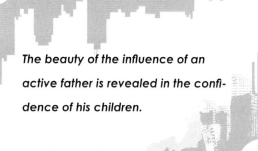

The beauty of the influence of an active father is revealed in the confidence of his children.

get my hands dirty to build a fortress to live in, I can just wake up, stretch out my arms, take a deep breath and bask in the glory that my father creates for me. Who says I have to do it all on my own? I've got a father who is willing to do a good portion of it for me!"

Fathers are to be strength in spite of weak moments, as exemplified by their unwavering commitment and they must be strong enough to tackle any bear or giant! The fathered child believes, "World-class wrestlers have no chance when it comes to defeating my father!" The image of a father flexing his bicep and kids jumping up to see how long they can hang on is the physical image of the emotional strength fathers invest in their kids. "You can hang on to me and I won't let you fall." "You can jump up and grab hold, and I won't be too hard for you to reach. I'll swing you, and although it might be uncomfortable at times, trust me, I'll never let you fall."

When they're home, there's an atmosphere of peace, safety and tranquility that supersedes everything else that may have been present while he was away. Nobody makes mama smile like he can because fathers are Casanovas and know just the right words to say. Every father must be able to sing and even if they can't, when they sing, it sounds good to us.

But in all seriousness, fathers can see what we can't see and they have the wisdom to prepare us for it before we even know what's coming. Fathers possess a vision that could only have been given to them by God. Vision beyond what their eyes could perceive or their ears could hear. They have an ability to make the intangible tangible. Fathers ensure we don't get lost in the whirlwind of life or swept away by the tornadoes of trouble. They make sure we are fully prepared when the floods of despair attempt to overwhelm us. They literally yell, "Watch out!" before adversity even begins to come our way. They have the uncanny ability to see with their eyes closed and to dream when the world waits to visualize the invisible.

Fathers are master directors - like the conductor of a legendary orchestra. Every instrument works separately, yet together to create one sound that is both beautiful and harmonious. Each horn and stringed instrument would be in complete discord if not for the conductor's ability to speak to each musician with a single movement, saying one thing with diverse meanings. The conductor moves once, but conveys several things to several different people at the same time. The conductor is smooth yet abrupt, big yet not incomprehensible, strong but fair, extremely demanding yet worthy of respect.

This is a father - one who knows how to lead and who we are completely willing to follow. In a dark and weary land, fathers represent light and a path for our feet. When the winds are blowing and we can hear the leaves but can't see the trees, no one is afraid because they know that their father is there. When a father takes you through a dark place you're still encouraged because you know that dark place will eventually give way to a place of light and glorious accomplishment. A father's intent is to never lead you down the wrong path. A father is a wise man of astute counsel.

CHAPTER 3:

THROUGH THE EYES OF GOD

Not everyone is fit to father you. It takes a special person to be aware of your vulnerability and not take advantage of it. It requires a high degree of both maturity and integrity to know that you can but don't, know you could but won't, and to do what's best and not just what's best for you! Fathers are intended to be the example of God's love, protection and provision manifested on earth. There is a void in mankind's heart that only our Heavenly Father can fill! Likewise, there is a void in every man's heart that only their earthly father can fill! For this reason fatherlessness has eroded the fiber of

Fathers are intended to be the example of God's love, protection and provision manifested on earth.

the human family structure! Fatherlessness is adverse to God's will!

In order to understand fatherhood from God's perspective we've got to understand relationship, and the most important relationship we must consider is our relationship with God, our father. Earthly fathers represent to their sons and daughters what our heavenly father represents to all of us. Earthly fathers, just like our heavenly father, represent a safe place. Fathers provide natural, spiritual and emotional nourishment. Fathers give us vision, direction, clear our path and create an environment where we can thrive. Understand this: God is love. Everything that God does, He does from a place of love. Every rebuke is because He loves us. Every trial He allows us to endure is because He loves us. Every triumph He allows us to experience is all because He loves us. God is love, and fathers are the representatives of that love on earth.

Fathers are the first pastors and spiritual leaders of the home. They are intended to be an exact embodiment of what God desires. Fathers are meant to be a type of Christ to their children; redeemers to those who have lost their way, deliverers to those who are entangled in unproductive behaviors, healers to those who may be suffering from emotional wounds to which medicine cannot minister, and shepherds of their own flock, traveling to the beat of their own drum going in the direction that was strategically prepared for them. Christ loved the church. He loved

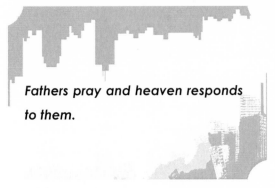

Fathers pray and heaven responds to them.

the church so much He gave himself for it (Ephesians 5:25). This investment is given freely. It does not have to be earned, there's no cost associated with it. It is given because of the care and concern in the heart of the Giver. Fathers introduce the word of God, and as a result, their words make more sense because they sound like God. Fathers pray and heaven responds to them. In order to understand the role of a father, from God's perspective, we must understand love and its role in our lives. Love is an extremely complicated emotion - difficult both to master and to understand. Thousands of books have been written to try and explain it. Tens of thousands of proverbs have been recited trying to express it and millions of songs have been sung hoping to evoke it!

If Love could speak or if Love were a person, he would probably feel lonely and misunderstood. He would feel manipulated because he had been used to fulfill selfish and sometimes malicious ambitions. He would feel taken advantage of, used and left for dead. He would feel like he was standing alone, when he wants nothing more than to be engulfed in an intimate conversation with someone, anyone, to explain how he sees the world while simultaneously accepting the opposite world perspective. He would be willing to have in-depth conversations with people he didn't agree with. He would readily accept people whose lifestyle, in his opinion, was unacceptable. He would respect people who were not considered respectable. Inevitably he would love people who were not lovable! He would be one of the most misunderstood people in every circle or environment he found himself in. Nobody would understand why he would smile and nod while painfully disagreeing. "Why", it would be asked, "does he tolerate people who attempt to manipulate and misuse him?" "He's crazy", some would say. He'd have no racial bias or prejudice, he would not be driven by competitive unction or selfish ambition. His heart would always be on display and although everyone could see it, feel it, hear it, touch it, no one could turn its affection from them, even if they wanted to.

People would say, "I know he feels like he's always right, regardless of the circumstances but he never tries to prove it". Many would hate him because he's so stubborn and never changes his mind. "He's so weak", some would say. They would say that because he knows everybody's darkest secrets but he plays dumb, like he doesn't know anything! Many of us would say things like, "I just don't understand him. I don't really like how he makes me feel, I just don't get him and sometimes I downright hate him!" I can't live without him, trust me I've tried. Love is the lone blanket accessible to you in a desolate and barren land on a cold dark night. It has the ability to comfort you when all other prevailing circum-

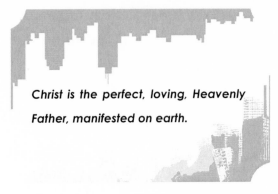

Christ is the perfect, loving, Heavenly Father, manifested on earth.

stances offer nothing more than adversity.

Now realize that Love is not just a hypothetical person. Love is Jesus Christ and Jesus is Love! Christ is the perfect, loving, Heavenly Father, manifested on earth. The example we should all follow!

PART TWO

HOW FATHERLESSNESS AFFECTED MY NATURAL MAN

CHAPTER 4:

I RESENTED MEN IN AUTHORITY

The "I'm my own man" mentality started early in my life. As a little boy, making friends came very easily to me. I was so energetic and always looking for some trouble to get into! In the third grade I realized girls liked me and I would instinctively come up with ways to agitate every girl I could. Pulling ponytails hitting and running and name calling were my go-to moves. This behavior, however, quickly presented a problem for me, I ALWAYS ended up in trouble with the teacher!

All my life to this point I had become accustomed to women as authority figures. In hindsight I realize that I developed a level of comfort with women that I did not have with men. Although I was initially disobedient, I respected my female teachers and acknowledged when they corrected that disobedience. I rarely talked back, and when I did ,it was laced with an attempt to charm my way out of the trouble I most certainly created. I responded, in the most healthy way I could, because there was a familiarity with them that they didn't have to earn. Maybe they subconsciously reminded me of my mother.

The first day of fourth grade was something I'll never forget! The school year started off with a blast. I was wearing my ONLY new school outfit for the first time and I felt like a million bucks! I remember leaving the house a little early that day to meet my best friends at the corner to start the festivities. We were blessed, in that there were many cute girls in our neighborhood, so the walk to and from school was always an adventure! We started our routine of hit and run, pinch and pull and whatever else we could think of and it lasted all the way to school. After a quick breakfast, consisting of a super donut and either orange juice in the green and orange container or vitamin D milk in the blue and white cardboard container. This breakfast was essentially a sugar blast for, in my case, an already overly active kid!

I walked into my classroom for the first time that year and noticed that my teacher was an older male. I distinctly remember thinking "I don't want him to be my teacher"! It was not until much later in life that I realized why the sight of this male teacher ruined my perfect first day of school! I had a disdain for older men, especially an older man I didn't know. I was committed to showing everybody that nobody could tell me what to do. I felt it was my responsibility to prove to other men that I was strong and I couldn't be bullied. I never had a man to teach me how to get girls,

ride a bike, play sports, or anything else that I had participated in and I didn't need one now. I carried that sentiment throughout my youth, into my adult life.

So here I was with this male teacher who didn't seem
like he'd be giving me any special favors and he'd expect
me to be OK with that. I made it up in my mind that day,
either they're going to give me a new teacher or I'll get
kicked out of this class. School is a place where children
are taught critical thinking, and the importance of healthy
communication skills, but I noticed from the very first time
I met that teacher that it was hard for me to think critical-
ly as I was consumed with unearned anger towards him.
When he asked me to do things I would blatantly ignore
him. When he tried to engage me to figure out what was
wrong I would lash out to show him I wasn't scared of him.

He tried to reason with me, yet I had an unreasonable
spirit towards him. "Steve," he would say, "can you read for
us the second chapter?" Far too often, I would respond, "I
can't read, and if I could I wouldn't read that!" I saw it as
a perfect chance to make people laugh, and at the same
time get on his nerves. I'd have an argument with my mother the night before, come to school and take my frustration out on him by refusing to listen and follow instructions.
I would yell, "I'm a grown man, I can take care of myself! I
don't have to do what you say!" But I was not grown, I was
not a man, and I couldn't take care of myself. In hindsight
I see how fatherlessness handicapped me by not allowing
me to receive instruction from good, responsible examples

of men. This teacher, as well as countless other male figures I encountered, had to suffer from the frustration in me, caused by one male figure I never even met.

I believe fathers have a God-given responsibility to establish respect. Fathers establish respect

In hindsight I see how fatherlessness handicapped me by not allowing me to receive instruction from good, responsible examples of men.

for self, respect for others and most importantly respect of consequences. When there is no father present to teach these invaluable principles, some children develop a tendency to progress through life without the ability to discern how impactful bad decisions can truly be. If I had a dollar for every time I yelled, "I DON'T CARE! AIN'T NOBODY GONNA DO NOTHING TO ME!" I would be beyond rich and wealthy. I sought out opportunities to be defiant. It became like a sport for me to push the envelope of disrespect when dealing with men I didn't know. My friends and I felt we WERE men, and what led us to believe that lie was the fact that we refused to listen and did not fear consequences. I resented my fatherless life, and I didn't know how to handle the emotions that I was carrying. My coping mechanism was anger.

CHAPTER 5:

I CONSTANTLY SOUGHT THE APPROVAL OF OTHERS

Children today are faced with challenges that generations before them never had to experience. The world has become so small. Everyone is accessible and everywhere is touchable. It is easy to be tricked into thinking you know someone. We watch an individual on TV and can immediately look them up by an endless number of internet options. Every outlet offers a different perspective of that person. We follow them on social media, watching and listening to them "up close". This access can mislead you into believing you really know that person! The problem is that you have never met them. Since you've never had a conversation with them or spent time with them, you can't really *know* them.

The reality is, there is a difference between what we do and who we are. We grow acquainted with the online or public persona that the person chooses to create or portray. However, the actual heartbeat of the person could be altogether different than the personality you identify with. This can be very dangerous to impressionable minds. It's easy to be attracted to their "lifestyle" and the feeling that their "lifestyle" evokes. It's even easier to subconsciously develop a value system based upon that perceived lifestyle.

We as human beings are hardwired to follow, and what we choose to follow can be the difference between success and failure - safety or hardship. Fathers naturally establish both good and bad standards and values in their children. Without the constant influence of a dedicated father, young, impressionable minds become vulnerable to outside examples and unfortunately

those outside examples are not always redeemable ones. Fatherhood is not a biological function only,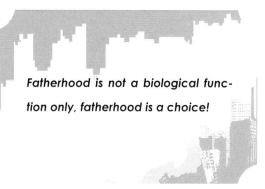

Fatherhood is not a biological function only, fatherhood is a choice!

fatherhood is a choice! It is intentional oversight and concern for the well-being of a seed. External examples are not always willing to accept the burden or responsibility that comes with being a role model. Even if they did, the role they want to model may not be trustworthy.

There is an endless number of voices telling us what life is supposed to be like. This makes the influence of a fully committed and concerned fatherly voice so important. It creates the trajectory of possibilities in the minds of their children. Without the benefit of that formative voice, I found myself searching, even when I didn't know what I was searching for! What's even more alarming is that I wasn't even aware that I was searching at all. I was searching with no direction; searching with no goal in mind; searching and finding nothing. Regardless, I was searching nonetheless.

I now realize I innocently desired something every human longs for...acceptance. Consequently an unnatural urge to prove my worth began to internally pressure me to fit into a mold that was not made for me. What mold, you might be wondering? I don't know! I don't know because it changed depending on the potential source of the acceptance. This behavior was extremely stressful! I had to be many people while being trapped in one person. I was a chameleon. I evolved to fit in or please those around me. Some may consider people who live like this as fake, but I disagree. A fake person is one who consciously and intentionally portrays one thing in an effort to deceive others. This was far from that!

I believe that everyone has an internal yearning to be accepted for who or what they are. Once acceptance is received the recipient can settle into the essence of themselves without wavering. Without the void of acceptance being filled, the individual has a tendency to self correct and adjust to what is expected of them. These adjustments are not in an effort to deceive anyone into believing they are something that they are not. On the contrary, this idiosyncratic behavior is an unconscious effort to find oneself. God placed deep down inside every one of us that acceptance is always applied to the purest version of ourselves. I have concluded that in the vast majority of cases people who find themselves constantly seeking or needing approval or acceptance may suffer from an identity crisis, as was the case for me.

I CONSTANTLY SOUGHT THE APPROVAL OF OTHERS

Maybe in some crazy way it worked both for good and bad in me at the same time. I travelled a diversity of roads and engaged in multiple activities that expanded my horizons. By experiencing all I could, I discovered that I was actually a pretty talented kid. Even though I was discovering all of these new and fascinating talents, I struggled to focus my attention on any given thing. I didn't know who I was nor was I aware of my purpose. I became preoccupied with being accepted as the "cool kid" despite the fact that at times other people liked the cool kid even more than the cool kid liked himself! Some might consider this sometimes controllable proclivity a weakness; an unnecessary vulnerability that could and should be avoided. Although I would agree on some level that it could and even should be avoided, I would like to add a strain of perspective to the contrary. True weakness is an unwillingness to acknowledge weakness. Being too proud to admit and bring awareness to one's flaws is dangerous.

I've always said that a man who is unwilling to admit he has a problem will never fix it! It takes a strong person to come to an awareness of themself. It then takes courage to be willing to challenge yourself to improve. In pursuit of the better version of yourself, you'll learn it's not even realistic to expect to be accepted by everyone. You must learn, as I did, that you are uniquely designed by God and you are picture perfect just as you are. Ultimately there are only two sources of acceptance you absolutely need - God and yourself! Everything and everyone else is just icing on the cake of life.

CHAPTER 6:

I SOUGHT UNHEALTHY SUBSTITUTES FOR FAMILY STRUCTURE

Fathers create unspoken boundaries by their presence alone and as a child, I had NO boundaries. I'm still amazed by the things I got away with and that my mother never knew about *until now*. I remember one particular late night, maybe Friday or Saturday, when I was about 13 years old. Generally the real fun started after 10 pm. The air was cold enough to wear our favorite starter jacket but also warm enough for us to be comfortable hanging outside all night long. I had on one of the leather jackets I was known for wearing. I would regularly choose one of my leather jackets over my starter coat because at the time EVERYBODY and a few more people wore starter jackets and I loved to be different. I always wanted to stand out!

My friends and I secured a ride to the Jammy Jam, one of the best teenage parties around! Wherever we went, there was always at least five of us and we called ourselves "Simply Dōp." We also had a bunch of really close friends from different neighborhoods around the city and when we all got together trouble was imminent. We had this twisted idea that fighting was fun and only the people who were willing to fight and risk everything were truly "family". We arrived at about 10:30 pm, the perfect time to get on stage and win the dance contest, as usual! We came, we conquered and after receiving our prizes, we commenced to Jammy Jamming the night away! The Jammy Jams were notoriously fun and entertaining, but every Jammy Jam had to come to an end.

The songs began to slow down as the DJ worked to mentally prepare us for what they hoped would be a swift departure. During the traditional two-step slow dance, one that every junior high student had to master, the lights began to flicker on one at a time. Back then, the only people who left parties early were the people whose parents picked them up and were determined to beat the "after party rush". Nobody wanted to leave early because the end of that party was the beginning of a new party - the fight party!

Once the lights were on, our mission was to get as many girls' phone numbers as we could while looking for new ways to entertain ourselves. The competition between boys, person to person and crew to crew at this time proved to be at its zenith! Instinctively we became highly sensitive to any form of perceived disrespect from our rivals. The primary goal was to look out for self, but there was also the responsibility to look out for your "family". If any individual was unwilling to sacrifice their own safety and even freedom for the benefit of the family, they were considered unfit to be "family" altogether. Even if the danger was justifiably caused by that family member, you still had to be willing to risk all to defend them.

As we spilled out into the parking lot under the cover of darkness, trouble ensued. That particular night tensions were extremely high and the congregation of partygoers was a smorgasbord of neighborhood mixes. This was the perfect ingredient for a violent preteen tsunami! At times, fights broke out and everyone would participate in the swinging and kicking and most of the people involved wouldn't even know the reason for the fight in the first place. This was the case that night. The fight consumed the banquet hall's parking lot and soon spilled out into the intersection.

One street was Little Richmond, a side street. The other street, Gettysburg, presented the most eminent danger. It is one of the most traveled main thoroughfares in the entire city! Both streets were blocked by youngsters fighting, yelling, arguing and watching. Traffic was backed up for what seemed like miles. (I can't be sure because I was kinda occupied.) After these experiences the family would huddle together in fellowship at the residence of choice and discuss the festivities. We would rehearse the whole event from beginning to end.

This is the time when people would be enlightened on how it all started, for all who didn't know but participated anyway. We would start at the beginning and slowly work our way back to the end, over and over again for what seemed like forever. Everyone had a different perspective and nuance to their story. We would make sure to stop at every point and highlight all of the funny moments! It was shocking how, in such a serious set of circumstances, we were able to find so much to laugh about. During the post game huddle we also identified moments we felt like someone didn't hold up their end of the bargain. Likewise we highlighted The Honorable Moments of our brothers.

It may sound trivial to an outsider, but serious implications came out of the details of these meetings! If an individual had constantly shown "selfish tendencies" like running for safety, disappearing during the heat of the battle or giving any impression they were not sold out for the cause, they could be excommunicated forever! The community is so much more complex than I have time to explain. There were times when an individual didn't live up to the fundamental expectations of the family, but they failed to, not because they wouldn't, but because they couldn't, they would be covered and protected instead of cast away. These run-ins with "other families" were necessary because they revealed to everyone the most solid family members, which would in turn establish an unspoken hierarchy amongst the brotherhood. Skirmishes with others were one of the most effective ways to earn the respect of your peers. Our perspective was simple, if I can't trust you when I'm in trouble I can't trust you at all!

The lack of a father figure rendered my family structure unstable and unbalanced. Due to the absence of a father, my mother had to work when she should've been able to rest, therefore my home lacked social interaction and rela-

Often times unhealthy relationships are fed and made possible by the unhealthy family structures fatherless children grow up in!

tionship-building opportunities. My home lacked affirmation. My home lacked accountability. These are the ingredients required to create the perfect storm for gangs, as well as many other unhealthy relationships. Often times unhealthy relationships are fed and made possible by the unhealthy family structures fatherless children grow up in! My other family, my street family, gave me all of the things my home life was missing and relationships were forged for life during moments just like that night at the Jammy Jam.

I SOUGHT UNHEALTHY SUBSTITUTES FOR FAMILY STRUCTURE

POSITIVELY

CHAPTER 7:

I BECAME DETERMINED TO PROVE EVERYBODY WRONG

I attended Patterson High School. For me, school was more about fun than about books. Even though I wasn't a good student, I always loved going to school because that's where all the fun happened. I especially loved pep rallies. I vividly remember one pep rally my sophomore year. The day started off like every other day started for me-in trouble, but the good kind of trouble. The kind of trouble that made everybody else laugh, or at least that was my goal. As the day progressed and it got closer to the pep rally, the excitement of not having to go to class began to overwhelm me. When the time finally came, I couldn't wait to get down to the gym!

As usual, I pressed my way through the crowd to make sure I got the best seat in the house! I was sitting right at mid court, about halfway back so I could see the entire gym, the entire floor and everybody who was coming and going. That was important because anything could happen and I wanted to see everything. There also had to be cute girls in front of me, behind me, and on both sides of me or else it wouldn't have been right! Immediately the fun started! I picked out everyone who caught my attention and I talked about them until everybody was laughing. My regular joking opponents joined in and we talked about each other in an attempt to make sure during the entire pep rally everybody would succumb to laughter.

One joke I made caught the attention of one of the young ladies sitting next to me and she didn't like it. The pep rally was an in-school wrestling match - our team against the visiting school. One of the guys on our team was getting beat pretty badly, badly enough that I couldn't stop talking about him. Now I wasn't talking about him in a demeaning way but I was talking about him in an "I'ma make everybody laugh at you" kind of way. This was normal. This was the culture of inner-city schools and maybe schools all over. I talked about him because he was losing. We laughed at him because he was losing bad and this girl, his girlfriend, was angry. She was so angry she challenged me. She exclaimed with all of the energy she could muster, "You couldn't do any better!" She yelled at me with her face turning red, pointing her finger at me with aggressive intent and said, "I bet if you wrestled you would lose every match"!

As a result of that challenge I discovered a sport that became a passion of mine for years to come! I immediately sought out the head coach of the wrestling team and told him that I was joining the team! He warned me against joining so late in the season because, "by now everybody else is ahead of you with their training and level of conditioning," he said. I responded without hesitation, "Coach, I'm joining! And I'm your new star"! I refused to delay the process. I was compelled to prove that girl wrong right now!

Ultimately I ended the season as a team captain and finished my two and a half year high school wrestling career as one of the best wrestlers in the entire state! I would have never accomplished even half of the amazing feats in my short wrestling career without that challenge. Her words were my greatest motivators when things got tough. When I found myself seemingly at my limit and questioned if I could go any further I heard her words and envisioned her feeling accomplished by seeing me fail. I imagined her pointing at me and it would give me a new burst of energy. She paved the way for my success by challenging me and not believing in me.

Very early on, that became the story of my life. Every major success was sparked by a challenge. The vehicle of resistance against me, whether tangible or invisible, was always real to me. Some of the resistance I was forced to overcome came from within. Internal questions about my ability would, at times, begin to grow and develop momentum and work against me. It's unbelievable how your own thoughts have the power to cripple your potential! The Holy Bible advises that we must be renewed by the renewing of our minds.

I BECAME DETERMINED TO PROVE EVERYBODY WRONG

I was plagued by questions of whether or not I even deserved better. The enemy from within has been the most difficult enemy to defeat! Although overcoming the enemy from within felt like a full-time occupation, that battle was just the beginning. To compound the difficulty of this internal struggle, there are also external walls to climb and barriers to burst through. Some people have a self-appointed anointing to identify everything that's too hard for you! I had to learn to be very careful about embracing the opinions of others concerning me. Not everybody who's with you is really *with* you. Some people are only close companions in certain seasons of your life be-

> *Some people are only close companions in certain seasons of your life because they are on assignment to derail your future.*

cause they are on assignment to derail your future. You must learn to be very careful of people who are always telling you what you can't do. Be advised, they are not always intentionally trying to derail you, sometimes people honestly believe you shouldn't or you couldn't because they didn't!

After learning this principle I became very selective with my choice of friends. I honestly can't pinpoint when it happened, but one day my perspective on adversity and difficulty shifted. I matured to a place where I embraced adversity

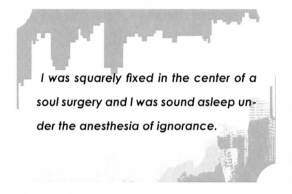

I was squarely fixed in the center of a soul surgery and I was sound asleep under the anesthesia of ignorance.

as a personal challenge. Hardship pushed me instead of discouraging me. God used the trials and tribulations of my childhood to develop this character quality in me and I was completely unaware. I was squarely fixed in the center of a soul surgery and I was sound asleep under the anesthesia of ignorance.

I consider this tendency, to feel challenged instead of discouraged, one of my greatest strengths! Literally the moment someone told me that I couldn't do something, that "something" would become a mission to accomplish! Being easily challenged while being unable to refuse an opportunity to prove someone wrong not only worked in my favor, it also worked against me! Thankfully, God used that same quality to set the course for my entire life, ministry and future.

I BECAME DETERMINED TO PROVE EVERYBODY WRONG

CHAPTER 8:

I BECAME A SELF-STARTER

I vividly remember fearlessly getting into constant trouble in school. I would argue with teachers, unnecessarily. Often times, I would use school as an opportunity to have fun, and to relieve stress. The constant threats from school administrators to call home almost always fell on deaf ears. I regularly pushed their patience to the limit, and put icing on top of my cake of disobedience by exclaiming, "You can call my mom, she ain't gone do nothing!" If my mother had become aware of my behavior, this would no doubt prove to be a lie! But I grew up in an era where there were no cell phones, no call waiting, and not everybody had answering machines; including us. Everybody had landlines or what we affectionately called "house phones".

In the homes of my peers, there were usually two phones that shared one phone line. One rotary phone would be hung on the wall in the kitchen, usually next to the dining area. The second phone would be located in the front room next to the couch. This was also the case in our home for my entire childhood. The fact that the phones shared a line is significant- because when the administrators threatened to call home, I proceeded to slightly pull the phone in the front room off the hook. This would ensure that if and when the school called home, the phone never rang on our end! This among other tactics, such as failing to bring letters home, while simultaneously checking the mailbox in case they sent anything through the mail actually kept my mother in the dark concerning my errant behavior.

Contrary to what I said to the administrators, my mother was anything but an unconcerned parent! She was fully invested in the well-being of her children like no other! The problem was, she was forced to work unrealistic jobs, shifts and hours just to provide the basic necessities for her family. For as long as I can garner a memory, my mother worked two and three jobs faithfully yet her income never seemed to be enough! Looking back and considering the sacrifices she tirelessly made, I have to say that MY MOTHER IS SUPERWOMAN!

My earliest memories are of having to accept that my mother was rarely home. When she

MY MOTHER IS SUPERWOMAN!

was home those few hours were spent sleeping. She was always under pressure to recover quickly because she constantly ran from one job to another, often on public transportation. She was either awake at work or asleep at home and this was her life. She was instinctively selfless! I can't remember her buying herself anything. Her concern was always zeroed in on my sister and I. The pressures of providing a stable roof over our heads didn't allow her the luxury of sharing her life with the very children she was providing for, yet she never complained - she continued!

As a child with very little supervision and an abundance of excess time on my hands I developed dreamer tendencies. What I'm referring to as" dreamer tendencies" are the inherent creative abilities that every child possesses. The difference in how they're utilized seem to drastically differ for rich kids and poor kids and I was on the side of the materially deprived. Obviously, this is a generalization based upon my limited observation, but most poor kids and rich kids appear to focus their God-given creative juices differently. Many rich kids are afforded the luxury of imagining amazing things beyond this world - things that most would consider purely based in fantasy and fiction. I, on the other hand, occupied countless hours dreaming about the possibility of my reality changing. My dreams were not fantasy or fiction but they were my future reality. I held on to the idea that life could, should and eventually WOULD be better for me!

My dreams became my constant motivation! My dreams were aggressive taskmasters that would not let me rest. My dreams and my lack of material possessions, working together, provided me with the building blocks I needed to become a self-starter. I developed a reputation amongst my peers for being a doer. I was willing to be a habitual risk taker. I was not blessed with a visible or tangible example of how my dreams should be realized, so I became the embodiment of spontaneity. I was driven by my desire to obtain the things that seemed out of my reach. I became a result seeker! I knew life should, could and would be better, so I refused to wait on anybody to push me or reassure me. As a result of the unique ingredients of my childhood, I became a self-proclaimed self starter.

CHAPTER 9:

I GAINED CONFIDENCE IN MY GIFTS AND ABILITIES

Throughout my childhood I repeatedly made the mistake of attributing everything that increased my confidence to some external stimuli. In hindsight, I'm convinced my confidence barometer was broken. It wasn't broken because I constantly lacked confidence; it was broken because I never found the ability to regularly believe in myself by myself without any external influence. It was broken because it was so inconsistent! I remember seasons in my life when I oozed confidence! I was so over-the-top confident that I could pass out pounds of it to charity and still have more left over than I would ever need. Confidence, at times, was such a rich resource at my fingertips; the sheer abundance of it would make many people uncomfortable. It could regularly be misinterpreted as cockiness. There were just seasons of my life where I simply believed in myself in any and every way.

I GAINED CONFIDENCE IN MY GIFTS AND ABILITIES

During these times, I lived on the most vertical peak of the highest mountain. Losing was not an option, and nobody could deny me!

But, there were an equal number of seasons where I wished I could disappear - times when hiding was my method of coping. Shrinking in an effort not to stand out in any way was the agenda. I felt so self-conscious I couldn't find any peace! I was critical to the point of crippling myself. At those times I didn't like my look, and I felt I was too short and that my nose was too big. I thought my cheeks were too pinchable or that I looked too young. I didn't like my name and hated my voice on recordings! This was devastating to me, especially since I felt destined to be a rap star!

This constant dichotomy was the result of a broken confidence barometer. I swung from one end of the pendulum to the next. It would be a gross understatement to say my confidence was high one day and low the next. It was more like it transcended all upward boundaries: shattering all tangible ceilings with the speed, force and trajectory of a meteor...one moment. The next moment my complete lack of confidence could be characterized as lower than the depths of a bottomless pit beneath the ocean floor! Yes, it got that low. At times, this was not just the case from day to day, but from moment-to-moment. My constantly changing emotional state resulted in regular mood swings, affected my every thought and left me disturbingly indecisive and this up-and-down demeanor was constantly fed from

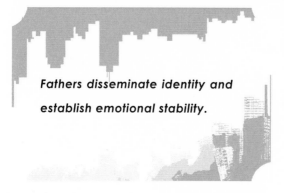

Fathers disseminate identity and establish emotional stability.

the plate of inconsistency.

Fathers disseminate identity and establish emotional stability. My father's absence was even more destructive than I ever knew for this and so many other reasons! One primary reason is that this missing relationship caused me to lean and depend on people, places and things that regularly left me disappointed. The disappointment was largely because I was trying to fill the void my father's absence created. All of those people, places and things added value to my life in different ways, but they were never meant to offer me the self-sufficiency a father is responsible for. Eventually, I grew weary of being disappointed by things I couldn't control and it was very rarely the fault of the "thing". The real issue was the fact that I was expecting something that these people, places, and things were unable to provide.

The constant frustration caused by my circumstances, slowly led to a life-changing self discovery. I was special! Until this point, I was so focused on my environment and what was missing, that I was unable to see myself clearly. I began to realize that I had unique qualities, gifts and talents that would shine through with little to no intentional effort. This discovery of the me that was always there awakened a curiosity about myself. I quietly thought about the potential that I possessed and whether or not this newfound uniqueness was real or just a figment of my imagination. Could I really be this special?

I began to challenge myself to be me and not just what I thought people wanted me to be. Initially, this was difficult. It's almost impossible for someone to be authentically themselves if they don't even know who they are. But fortunately for us all, the real, uncompromised you is deep down at the core of who you are and has always been there! When I was a young minister, the Lord spoke life-shaping words into my spirit at a time when I found myself questioning my call to servanthood. These words embody this principle perfectly. The Lord spoke clearly, "You are what I say you are, even if you're not it yet"! The Holy Bible declares, "*Before I formed you in the womb I knew you, and before you were born I consecrated you; I appointed you a prophet to the nations.*" Jeremiah 1:5 (ESV).

Boy, do I wish I was aware of this principle earlier in life. It would have saved me so much self-inflicted emotional trauma! As I began to explore the

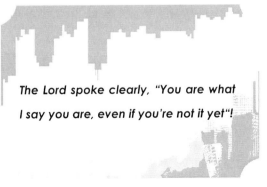

The Lord spoke clearly, "You are what I say you are, even if you're not it yet"!

newfound version of me, amazing things started to happen. I tested my gifts and   talents one at a time, usually reluctantly. To my surprise, it generally worked out better than I secretly expected. The favor of God rested on the gifts he instilled in me but I was still unaware of what was actually taking place. I was essentially an innocent bystander with a secondhand perspective watching God empower me simply by me being me!

I quickly learned that the only thing I could control with any regularity was myself. I slowly flirted with leaning on the things that make me who I am and the results were remarkable! Instead of being overly critical of the quirks in my personality, I became unapologetically me and was amazed to find that people liked the real me even better than the counterfeit me that I had created. As I learned to lean on my own gifts and talents, I taught myself to accept myself. Yes, I'm weird but I learned to love it. Yes, I'm goofy, but I learned to love it. I'm a lot of things and I systematically learned to love myself completely! It wasn't until I began to trust my instincts that I was able to start seeing certain things settle.

The power that the world had over me to manipulate my emotional stability grew weaker. The external factors that once had so much control over how I saw myself began to lose their mojo. I eventually grew to a place of elite confidence when I realized, God made me this way, I accept it and I like it. This became the proverbial get out of jail free card every time life challenged me. Nothing or nobody could convince me of anything contrary to what I inadvertently discovered...ME! I didn't yet have an intentional relationship with God, but I knew- somehow- that God made me special. It was this realization that purchased the lenses that I would come to see the world through from that point forward. He put gifts in me and by finally being myself, I tapped into those gifts and stepped into empowerment. I was not more special than anybody else, but I was uniquely special- different from everybody else. Different for a reason, even though I didn't know the reason yet. The inconsistencies around me challenged me to look within; finding the me that had been hiding there the whole time!

The inconsistencies around me challenged me to look within; finding the me that had been hiding there the whole time!

THE FATHERLESS SON

PART THREE

HOW FATHERLESSNESS AFFECTED MY SPIRITUAL MAN

CHAPTER 10:

I BEGAN TO CLING TO FATHER FIGURES

I found that growing up without a father is the best acting coach any aspiring actor could ever ask for. It teaches you to suppress the natural desire for a father-child relationship. It quickly becomes second nature to hide pain, and simply play nonchalant like you couldn't care less. But I cared. I *care*. And it's okay to care.

Fathers have a responsibility to develop strong independent thinkers who can survive the   turbulence of life. Leaving the growth and development of a young mind and spirit to chaos and chance is so wrong, for so many reasons! Men who leave the responsibility of raising

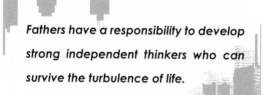

Fathers have a responsibility to develop strong independent thinkers who can survive the turbulence of life.

their children to someone else is not a father, but more of a caricature. This is not said in an effort to

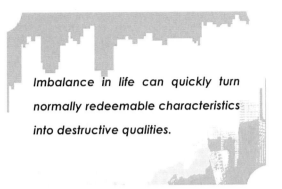

Imbalance in life can quickly turn normally redeemable characteristics into destructive qualities.

demean or cast away. There's help for absent fathers, just like there's help for the real victims...the children, but that's not the focus of this book.

Any malleable substance molded by unintentional sculpting will potentially have unintended deformities. I suppressed my ever deepening desire for a father-son relationship for so long, that I innately overcompensated whenever I was introduced to any seemingly suitable father figure. Maybe it was my subconscious self fervently trying to prove that I could be an honorable son. Imbalance in life can quickly turn normally redeemable characteristics into destructive qualities. As a father myself, I feel honored when my kids hang on to my words and the sound of my voice. I encourage them to listen intently. It could one day be the difference between life and sudden death!

Fatherlessness can leave you so wounded in so many ways even the wounded don't recognize it. Unrelenting emotional stress over an extended period of time will eventually take its toll. Soldiers who remain in harm's way during times of war without regular relief exhibit symptoms of post traumatic stress disorder, or PTSD, a psychological term popularized in recent years. This condition influences the world view of a person. It has such a powerful impression on one's worldview it can literally cause a person to make decisions that they wouldn't make under normal circumstances. This, in my opinion, is an aggressive example of the daunting effect fatherlessness has on so many people I know, including me!

That endless emotional void pushed me to a point where I lacked balance. I gravitated to any father figure I could find. I became fixated on being around them. Wanting to be rid of the void in my spirit as quickly as possible, I attempted to make up for lost time. The continuous desire to have a father fill-in for my absent father made me vulnerable to the aspirations of others. I had one desire: to be instrumental in the fulfillment of the vision of whichever father figure I was attached to at any given time. In the spirit, I was like a "hip baby", attached at the hip and always wanting to be attached, and I was proud of it! The treacherous element of that mentality is, I was a son that had never been fathered - a son who lacked balance. Therefore, I was unable to discern how to serve honorably with balance and individuality.

I unknowingly absorbed everything, but lacked the ability to eat the meat and throw away the bone. Instead of absorbing spiritually and socially redeemable qualities and rejecting everything unfit for my health, wealth and spiritual growth, I consumed everything. Being unintentional about separating the good from the bad, left me susceptible to being used, manipulated and even at times, emotionally abused. And although it's not my testimony, I believe this is one reason why children become victims; not only to emotional abuse, but every kind of unthinkable abuse, at the hands of men they trust! It's honorable and even advisable for a child to stick close to the heart of the father.

A healthy father-child relationship teaches a child how to benefit from the father. Most importantly it teaches them how to lean on God! You may be very similar to your father in appearance, word and deed, but you are still uniquely you! Clinging so closely that I lost the ability to be myself and to respect the difference between right and wrong was the result of developmental deformities. I had to learn how to be close but not clingy. To be loyal to my father, but not dishonorable to God. To emulate his righteous ways but not repeat his mistakes.

CHAPTER 11:

I ATTEMPTED TO BE A CLONE OF MY SPIRITUAL FATHER

Sitting in the sanctuary patiently waiting for the last counseling sessions to be over and for everybody but the brethren to leave so I could spend quality time with my "father"- those moments were the highlight of my life! I asked every question I could about his childhood and his early school days and especially his ministerial upbringing. As much as I truly wanted to genuinely know about him, there was also a selfish component to my questioning. I wanted to compare my life to his, in an effort to search out the similarities down to the most minute details, because I found comfort in those similarities. The embarrassing fact was, I was essentially searching for an opportunity to say "Me, too, sir!!" I desperately wanted, *needed*, a "me too" moment with my father!

I asked, "What did you like about your childhood growing up?" "What was your favorite part about ministry?" "What did you used to read?" "How do you feel about racism?" "What do you think about this person's legacy?" "What stood out to you about them?" It seemed like I would never run out of questions. I imagine it must have been exhausting! I measured my potential in ministry based on how much my story matched his. I observed details as miniscule as his shoes. In my mind I'd think, "I'm going to wear shoes just like that one day." I attempted to become interested in things outside of my normal sphere of interest to be able to say we were just alike! As false as that narrative was, I worked tirelessly to at least convince myself, even if nobody else could see it!

As embarrassing as it is to admit today, I became a child around him. It felt almost like I found my place, when I became that sponge, that maybe I should have been as an adolescent. It also became a tremendous burden because like a child, I unconsciously became dependent on his approval. I mean, I didn't want to do ANYTHING without running it past him first. It almost became so egregious that, sometimes, I wonder if I BELIEVED I could accomplish anything without his approval!

I became so dependent that I literally found myself searching for my identity in him, and had to be an exact clone of him. If I didn't look like him, it would begin to frustrate me because I internalized it and convinced myself that it was because something was wrong with me. I would look at my brethren in ministry and attempt to identify how they looked like him, and how they were similar to him. I wanted to know if I was absorbing the characteristics, mannerisms and ideologies that they were obtaining, and if not, why? I measured my quality as a man and as a minister on the number of boxes I could check on the "how I stacked up to him" chart.

I don't know how many years it took for me to realize that as long as I attempted to be him I could never master being *me*. During those years I failed to really sharpen the unique me because I was too busy trying to become the me I wanted to be, and the me I wanted to be was *him*. I wasted years of my life and ministry trying to sound like him, move, eat, breathe and think like him. This is not to say that his fingerprint is not on the DNA of my development, because it most certainly is! However, the Lord put him in my life to shape me, not for me to be or attempt to become him.

My spiritual father was not a bad man, but he was just a man. No matter how much I admired him, no matter how much I looked up to him, regardless of how much I was attracted to the unique qualities that made him him, I could never master being him and God didn't expect me to. It wasn't until I realized that I wasn't approaching my development in a healthy way, that I began to see the unhealthy character flaws that I had developed along my journey. My perspective became poisoned with self-righteousness. I saw people through the lens of the immature underdeveloped man I was, expecting everybody to do things the same way my spiritual father did. Obviously, that's not possible, and it's not even God's will.

I was met with so many different methodologies that I didn't approve of, because in my mind, if you weren't doing things the way we did them, then you weren't doing anything at all! This is the worst mentality anybody could have when it comes to ministry and sadly enough, I must admit, this mentality is what I mastered. I wasn't seeing through a glass darkly - I question whether I was seeing at all. I measured every pastor by the yard stick of my own pastor. I measured every relationship by the dynamics of this sometimes dysfunctional father-son relationship, and I came to certain conclusions; not based upon my own ability to think, but based upon, "what would my father think?".

As a black man, it is painful to be judged by the poisonous perspective of an unaware bystander instead of the content of your own character. But, sadly, this was a principle that I disobeyed over and over again. I repeatedly judged people, places, and things based upon how alike or different they were from my environment. Some people will ask, "what's wrong with that?" Truth will tell us that not every environment is the same, not every circumstance is the same, not every relationship will look alike- and that's okay. The wonderful reality is that "different" does not equal "wrong" - "different" simply means "different" and that's it.

At times I wonder if that would've been such a hard concept for me

> *As a black man, it is painful to be judged by the poisonous perspective of an unaware bystander instead of the content of your own character.*

to grasp if I'd simply had balance! The apostle Paul made a statement, "follow me as I follow Christ" (1 Corinthians 11:1), implying that the follower can reach Jesus by imitating the leader as the leader selflessly strives for Christ! This is such a true and meaningful concept, but we must be careful not to fall into the trap of studying our teacher more than we study the word. I was so impressed with my pastor that I was distracted from the word. I listened to CDs of his sermons, I watched his DVDs. As I worked, his teaching played in the background. I fell asleep to recordings of him preaching, and I never missed a service.

I spent every moment that I could under his shadow and wing. I wonder now how much of that time I should have spent in prayer and fasting, and then studying the word on my own. Essentially, I developed a false sense of spiritual security. I felt strong when I was with him. I felt validated when I could share a "me, too" moment with him. But, I was not preparing myself for the inevitable time when I would no longer have him.

CHAPTER 12:

WHEN HE REJECTED ME I WAS COMPLETELY DEVASTATED
(OR, SO I THOUGHT)

One of the first things I learned as a pastor is that everybody grieves differently. There is no one way we must grieve. I've heard many people say experience is the best teacher, but I disagree. Experience is not the best teacher! It's the most expensive teacher. It's the most painful teacher, unfortunately, it's sometimes the only teacher a fool is willing to listen to! It's important to be willing to learn from other people's mistakes so that you don't

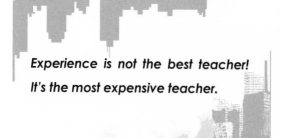

Experience is not the best teacher!
It's the most expensive teacher.

have to relive their mistakes and make your own, too. This principle may not be applicable in every difficult or painful circumstance, but it's definitely one that I've learned to live by.

One night in March of 2015, God woke me up out of my sleep and began to speak expressly into my spirit concerning the office of Pastor. I remember like it was yesterday! Chills shot through my body. Goosebumps rose beneath the surface of my thick skin. Through the hills and valleys of my elevated flesh the hair stood at attention like a ready Marine corps platoon! The house was still with sleep and peaceful darkness consumed every room. Although my eyes were closed, it seemed like I was glaring into the beaming light of a lighthouse in the midst of an immeasurable sea. I began to hear the voice of an Almighty and All-Knowing God. He spoke to me clearly concerning three primary areas of my next ministerial assignment.

First, the Lord revealed to me that I was being elevated to the office of Pastor. All of the guesswork was removed as He detailed my timeline and the steps I should take in order to transition fruitfully and faithfully. I was given a 10-month timetable. This immediately made me nervous, and my anxiousness questioned if what I had heard so clearly really came from the mouth of God - not because I was unsure I heard God's voice, but because I was sure my former pastor would respond negatively.

Second, the Lord revealed to me the name of my church. God reminded me of my primary gift in ministry;

the ability to restore people from brokenness. The Lord declared, "I have given you a unique ministry of Restoration and that is the name of your church, Restoration Church of Jesus Christ". I knew the name wouldn't be received well because no other Minister had ever gone out of our church to establish a church without keeping the same name!

Third, and most challenging, was the location of my next assignment. The Lord declared, "you are a son of this city and you have been called to restore and rebuild it". I was crushed by the anxiety I experienced thinking about having to tell my former pastor that not only was I leaving, but I was leaving and remaining in my hometown. We were always told that God would never send you out of a church and plant you in the same city. I became overwhelmed with stress at the thought of disappointing my spiritual father!

I dreaded the day I had to share with my former pastor the instructions the Lord downloaded into my spirit. No one ever left our church with anything less than a year's notice. Even one year was considered an extremely aggressive timetable. I was currently serving my local assembly faithfully as assistant pastor, and serving the body of Christ at large as an itinerant Evangelist. The latter was my ministerial dream, and I never seriously considered doing anything else. I was content with my scope of responsibility.

The Lord's instructions were completely wayward of the expected ministry etiquette I had been taught. Most people would consider this and the following things trivial, but if you've never experienced the thirst associated with wanting to please your father, you could never understand. The very thought of my former pastor being disappointed in me was catastrophic! Love makes you vulnerable. I loved my former pastor like he was my father, because at the time he was the only father that I had ever known. And although we have no connection now, I still genuinely love him.

I remember walking into his office to have that dreaded conversation and the agony I felt. After sharing with him everything that the Lord had revealed to me, I concluded with a statement that I believe was inspired by God himself: "As I prepare for my next assignment I only have one constantly pressing fear. I fear that if I decide to follow the will of God, it will leave me once again as a fatherless son!" After saying it I remember crying because it was such a pure representation of what was actually in my heart. What he said to me after my heartfelt confession was so hurtful, it's almost too embarrassing to share! I was devastated! He immediately responded, "You're not a pastor, you don't have what it takes, that's not God's will. You're going to destroy everything connected to you - your life, your family and your ministry"!

My remaining tenure was consumed with fasting and prayers asking God to convince my

God does not always give us what we want- regardless of how much we think we need it!

pastor not to reject me. I had to learn, however, that God does not always give us what we want- regardless of how much we think we need it! My former pastor never received my calling to the office of Pastor and openly declared that he rejected it repeatedly over the next several months, both privately and over the pulpit. That rejection of my ministerial assignment was accompanied by the intentional rejection of me as a son. Again and again, I was crushed!

I intended to remain in my former ministry through the end of 2015 with Watchnight (New Year's Eve) Service being my last, but about two weeks into October, Pastor called me into his office. He told me the last Sunday in October would be my last in that ministry. Despite the fact that I was destroyed by his rejection, I never advertised the fact that I was starting a church. I wanted to give my pastor the respect of telling his church, and I did not want him or anyone else to think I was evangelizing or attempting to recruit his congregation. I felt that it was my job to build that ministry until the day I left.

My last Sunday before departing, the last Sunday in October, began like most every other Sunday with the addition of all of the mixed emotions that came from something valuable ending, without the benefit of closure. It felt like a divorce and a funeral all at the same time. A divorce because I was being forced to separate from people whom I dearly loved. A funeral because I knew that the relational bonds that I built over the previous 16 plus years were evaporating right before my eyes. They were whispering away into eternity- never to be enjoyed again!

The entire sermon, just like many of the sermons that followed our initial conversation, was nothing more than another failed attempt at breaking my spirit and dimming my light. The service concluded in climactic fashion and my family's lives have never been the same since that day! My family and I were called to the altar. He began to speak over us. He declared, "Elder Saucer THINKS he's a pastor... but he don't have it. This is not God's will, he's going to curse everything connected to him - his family and his ministry because it's not God's will." He continued to speak concerning all the ways and reasons I was destined to fail. It felt as though tears were being crushed and squeezed out of each tear duct.

He continued by saying, "He's going to destroy everything around him; his family, his ministry and the lives of anyone who attempts to follow him. Therefore we will not be connected in any way. We will not be fellowshipping in any way. We will not help in any way, we're not even going to give him an offering!"

That was my last day as the assistant pastor of that church. Most importantly, that was the last memory I have concerning the relationship with, at that time, the only man I have ever called father. I was devastated! I was broken beyond repair...or so I thought!

Immediately after separating, I, at times, honestly thought I was losing my mental wellness. It impacted my ability to think clearly and function efficiently. In an effort to regain my footing, I attempted to maintain connections to whomever and whatever reminded me of him. Since I couldn't have him, I was determined to have a semblance of him, even if the connection wasn't a good fit. I attempted to brave the storm of turmoil my life had become but, at times, I felt like I just couldn't.

It wasn't until I found myself at an all time low, almost two years later, that God began to orchestrate meetings with another man of God. I saw him multiple times in various cities and events. Every time, he reached out to me and embraced me and my family. He saw something in me, but I had no idea why. So, initially, I resisted this relationship. I couldn't understand why this important man of God would be so willing to waste his time, energy and investment on me?

Then during the darkness of my emotional droughts, the Lord placed a scripture in my heart and the first clause of I Corinthians 4:15a (KJV) lit up before me! It declares, "*for though you have ten thousand instructors in Christ, yet you have not many fathers*". The revelation absorbed from that simple passage of scripture changed my life in a moment! "Not many" suggests that although true fathers are rare, you can be fathered by more than one man. Adoption from a dysfunctional family into a healthy family structure is the perfect natural example of this spiritual principle.

These encounters changed the course of my life physically, emotionally and most of all spiritually. Meeting this man of God reminded me of the one positive thing my former pastor said during that last tirade. As he stood me up with my family before the entire congregation and spoke the words that ripped my heart into pieces, there was a point when it was almost as though there was a battle of good and evil inside him. It seemed that after all of those years of faithful service the Lord wouldn't allow me to leave that place without validating my honorable stewardship to the assignment I had there. And as my former pastor spoke those words over me, he interrupted himself in the middle of the statement and declared, "out of all of the sons that have gone out of me, if I had to be honest, I couldn't send out a better Son". As I pondered those words, the Lord comforted my spirit, and   allowed me the privilege of being vulnerable again to a father. I stopped resisting the embrace of this new man of God.

POSITIVELY

CHAPTER 13:

I STROVE TO BE AN HONORABLE SON

I felt my life was worse off because of the absence of a man that I never even knew and it was difficult coming to grips with that reality. I set out on a mission to be an honorable son to anyone who would be willing to father me, but this was not a conscious decision of mine. Often times, people's behaviors (whether good or bad) are prompted by something much deeper, which was the case with my clinginess. I was a self-professed soldier for my "father". There was bliss associated with unquestioning loyalty! I remember thinking on many occasions "this is the kind of loyalty my father missed out on"! That one phrase fueled my tunnel vision concerning my familial commitment.

The day I revealed God's plan to my former pastor was tough. There were so many emotions working on me. It was a day full of extreme highs and lows. Considering I dedicated nearly 20 years of my adult life to this church, I found myself reminiscing about all of the memories - my children being christened on an altar I may never see again, getting married to the love of my life, suffering the loss of two babies; as well as houses, cars, businesses and more. It was the same place where the Lord raised us up and kept us whole in spite of it all! I kept thinking about being forced to disconnect from people with whom I thought I formed life-long bonds. My soul was being tortured by the thought of no longer having the comfort associated with maintaining those relationships.

It was a Bible study night and never, during the 16 plus years of attempting to serve God faithfully, was I more anxious in church. At one point in the service, I literally zoned out: seemingly floating in a space and time that became the defining moment of my forward trajectory. It was the day I woke up with an assignment to have a conversation exposing the depths of my heart and the exactness of the plans the Lord had downloaded into my spirit. I reluctantly approached the meeting, partly in fear that I and everything I had to say would be rejected. By this point in my life, my experiences had psychologically trained me to be accustomed to being rejected. Although it didn't hurt any less, I was used to it.

That day started just like every other day, except it was nothing like any other day. I woke up thinking, "Wow, this is the day I finally walk into manhood, a destination you don't arrive to until you're able to talk to your father, not just as a son, but as a man". I hear the questions ringing in your ears... "why would having a simple conversation about something the Lord said be so difficult"? The answer to that question is simple: I had never had such a substantive conversation with that level of conviction, in a man-to-man setting, with anyone who garnered that much respect from me. Ultimately, I was afraid he wouldn't approve of my future or believe in my vision. Sadly, I was right!

I vividly remember watching the clock and feeling like each second took five minutes to pass! I made the decision to fast and pray from the day I first received the revelation, until the day I shared it with my former pastor. So, in addition to being nervous, paranoid and anxious, I was tired, weak and hungry! I can honestly say I've never been more distracted sitting in a Bible study. My feet constantly tapping as if I was playing percussion instruments in my mind. No music yet my knees rhythmically bouncing was evidence of a subconscious nervous twitch that was seemingly beyond my control.

As service came to a close, I began to have a full conversation with myself. I began to rebuke myself! "Why are you so nervous? You're following God's will! You've finally arrived at the place in life where your existence has never been more meaningful"! As we finally made our way back to the office, my collar was soaked with perspiration. My nerves almost made my legs numb, yet my inherent courage began to grow as the words begin to form and force themselves out of my mouth! I didn't have to think about what I wanted to say, as the Holy Ghost began to show evidence of his control over me, and over that moment.

I began to explain all of the details concerning my future assignment. In that moment, I did not experience any anxiety, fear or nervousness. This would prove to be the same peace I would enjoy while walking in my purpose.

My nerves eventually returned for two reasons. First, as previously mentioned, everything the Lord showed me was unique in that it had never been done that way in that ministry. The name of my church was different, because everybody else just adopted a variation of the same name as the church they came out of. My timeline for transition was only officially 10 months, when everyone else who has ever transitioned did so in 12 to 24 months or more. No other churches from our organization ever shared a city. The unspoken expectation was that there was only supposed to be one church per city. However, I was compelled to follow the voice of God; and oh how I thank God I did!

The second reason was the weightiest and rang through my mind, heart and soul. As I finished sharing God's instruction and my interpretation of it, I shifted to sharing my heart. I explained my truth concerning my fatherless history as a reminder of why this was such a sensitive subject for me. I ended by stating, "I believe this is a test for both of us, but more for you than it is for me. This is because no matter what happens I will always maintain my respect for you. If you hate me, I'll love you. If you disrespect me, I'll maintain respect for you. I won't allow disagreement to change who I am, the way I carry myself or how I respond to you".

It was immediately obvious after sharing my vision,

that neither I nor my ministry would be received in that circle ever again! The average person might agree that the break up should have been an easy departure, but it's not as simple as it may seem. It became increasingly difficult to come to grips with the reality that I had invested so much in this relationship, yet I was forced to leave with nothing!

My entire life to that point was spent looking for a father I could be a son to. There was nothing in my life I was more obsessed with than being an honorable son, so this became a defining moment! Since I lacked a balanced son-to-father vantage point, I was unable to process his rejection healthily, despite the fact that I was being obedient to God's will. I began to internalize that rejection, believing that I must have done something wrong. I often teach that this is one of the most self-destructive things a person could ever do. You can never control the actions of others, you can only control how you respond to them. You give seasonal people unmitigated power over you when you internalize what they do and say.

You give seasonal people unmitigated power over you when you internalize what they do and say.

When you fully internalize this concept you will no longer berate yourself with thoughts like, "What's so wrong with me?" or "Is it something I've done?" You'll come to grips with the reality that people do whatever they want to do, and sometimes they're so selfishly motivated that they never consider how their words or actions might affect you. Essentially, I had to become one with the principle I teach everywhere I go: God will never hold you accountable for what people do to you, but he will always hold you accountable for how you respond to it!

Despite everything my former pastor said that final Sunday, there was one phrase uttered that allowed me to leave knowing that the Lord had heard my heart. One sentence that would unintentionally change the complexion of the moment for me and the trajectory of my future. He declared, " I'm leaving him in God's hands now." I was comforted because there are no better hands to be in! Thankfully, after that statement, none of his previous statements mattered. The Lord kept rehearsing in my spirit the words that were inspired by his approval over me. I learned a valuable lesson that day. Sometimes doing God's will does not involve convenience or comfort, only an assurance that He's ultimately in control: no matter how things turn out.

I was often embarrassed to admit that, as a grown man, I spent my entire ministerial life trying to not only please God, but my heart's desire was to also please my pastor. I had a picture of the road my life and ministry would travel, but God ultimately had a better plan for me! In recent years I've come to realize that God used one father to train me in the principles of sonship. Yet it was God's perfect plan to use those sonship intangibles to serve and add value to a different father. God sometimes has an unusual way of answering our prayers. My former pastor's rejection, initially so destructive, eventually lit a fire in me; refueling the desire to become an honorable son, but to the right father. My prayer has always been, "Lord let me be an honorable son and make my father proud". The Lord has answered my prayer!

CHAPTER 14:

I DEVELOPED THE STRENGTH TO SUBMIT TO CORRECTION, TRAINING AND DISCIPLINE

As far back as I can remember I recall making my favorite declaration, "My daddy taught me everything I need to know about how to be a man-to be nothing like him and everything he wasn't." Although this soothed my frustrations momentarily, it couldn't have been further from the truth! My father's absence actually reinforced all of the unhealthy behavioral patterns I had developed by observing and following the wrong examples. Without the structured discipline, and checks and balances that come with intentional fathering, I became masterfully undisciplined. Thankfully, something in me always pulled on me to be better. I knew, without knowing, that better was possible for me.

As I matured into a young adult, I quickly realized that if I really wanted to be better it would take an immeasurable amount of help. As a teenager it was as though I was exceptionally good at everything- except staying out of trouble! My senior year was no different, as I found myself potentially in trouble with the law once again. I was approached by a friend who told me the Marine Corps could be a positive alternative to facing the trouble I was in. That was all I needed to hear. Off to the Marine Corps I ran!

My decision to enlist was cemented by the fact that everybody I shared my intentions with became overwhelmed with disbelief. They assumed it was too tough a road for me to travel. Their reactions settled it. 90% of the reason I ultimately went in is because people thought I couldn't! I literally had no idea what I was getting myself into! But God's plan is always perfect and His strategies always work.

There was a particular drill instructor, Staff Sergeant Price, whom I was convinced hated me with a perfect hatred. He told me on one occasion that I could never lead his platoon in any capacity. I know now that he knew exactly what he was do- ing. With that

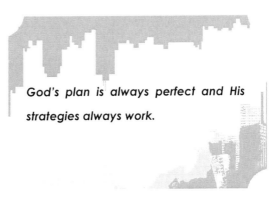

God's plan is always perfect and His strategies always work.

statement, and his perceived doubt in me, he lit an unquenchable fire in my spirit. That fire was the gasoline fueling the engine of my stick-to-itiveness! I determined, at that moment, that my personal mission would be to prove him wrong.

He would intentionally single me out for extra punishment and physical activity. As he saw my tolerance for this increase and my attention to detail become more evident he changed the game. I would get singled out for every little thing I did or didn't do. That quickly whipped me into shape and I became a model recruit. I was completely unprepared, however, for the wrinkles in strategy he would begin to employ. One day he made a declaration, "Recruit Saucer, since you're so tough, every time anybody in this platoon is out of order, out of position or commits a punishable offense, I want you to suffer and serve their punishment".

In almost every case the punishment was extra physical activity, which was so intensive that you usually were not finished until you had no more strength or energy left in your body. Initially, the way I processed it was to trick my mind into seeing him as my personal trainer. My body began to quickly change for the better so it was all worth

"adapt and overcome"

it to me, at first. Eventually paying for the deeds of others, for whom I did not feel responsible, got old. It got old real quick!

One lesson that I learned very early on in my Marine Corps training was "adapt and overcome". This proved to be the first time I would intentionally implement this principle. Neither my frustration with the situation nor my anger towards him had any positive impact on, what I perceived to be, his unfair and unjust treatment of me. It was not until I had an epiphany and realized I had to do something different if I wanted a different result.

Immediately, I began intentionally devoting energy into the entire platoon, one man at a time. My goal was to coach up each and every recruit, hoping to sharpen them and increase their preparedness. I realized, maybe 10,000 push-ups too late, that the key to less punishment was directly related to how well-trained my entire platoon was. Now my attention was no longer selfishly focused solely on my own well-being but rather on the competence of every marine involved! I eventually won the Staff Sergeant's trust and confidence, and was promoted to first squad leader. I graduated from Marine Corps Boot Camp at Parris Island, South Carolina as such.

After graduating Boot Camp, I eventually had the opportunity to speak to that drill instructor, not as a recruit in training but as a man and as a fellow Marine. With appreciation for his ability to shape me into a physical specimen, I looked him in his eyes and said, "Thank you, but at one point I honestly thought you hated me!" He immediately gathered himself with uprightness in his posture, only a marine would understand. He looked me in my eyes with a glassy glare, seeming to peer into the depths of my soul.

After about a minute of awkward silence, he spoke words into my spirit that would prove to set the course for the rest of my waking days! "Son" he said " when you came here you were oozing with leadership potential but you were not ready to lead. It was my job to see what was in you even if you couldn't see it and then pull it out of you! You were an excellent recruit but the platoon was in disarray. True leadership is when you can make everybody around you better by your presence and your influence. I used pain to focus your mind and discipline your body. Always remember no pain no gain, because pain is just weakness leaving the body!"

I continue to comfort myself to this day with those words. Nothing could break me because after enduring and conquering Marine Corps combat training I truly believed and believe, if I could make it through that I can make it through anything. Despite my experiences to that point, as impactful as they were, there was still only one primary driving force responsible for pushing me. The proverbial hand on my back, refusing to let me slow down or quit - the constant

True leadership is when you can make everybody around you better by your presence and your influence.

fear of becoming what I came from!

This is not in reference to my family in general, I have an amazing family! This is and has always been in reference to the one familial component that was my constant source of disappointment - the one component I lacked - my father. The Marine Corps was particularly effective in training my natural mind and body to conform to internal and external discipline. I personally credit the Marine Corps experience with preparing me for serving in the army of the Lord.

As a young pastor, I initially frustrated myself wrestling with the concept of why some people were so resistant to my leadership. The answer is multi-layered, and it cannot be fully addressed in this single chapter. I can, however, address a few things that resonated in my spirit after much prayer and searching God's heart for understanding.

Number one, I had to realize that not everyone that comes to class is a student. No matter how effective or sincere the efforts of the teacher, the student has a responsibility to come to class prepared to learn. If they're unprepared for class, they can't absorb what the teacher is imparting in others. They're too distracted by their own proclivities.

Likewise, not everybody comes to church for the same reasons. Some people have ulterior motives. Some people come with unspoken agendas. Some people are carrying so much trauma from the past that everything you say, everything you do and everything they experience will be filtered through the lens of what happened to them in their yesterday.

Number two, the people who need the most help are usually the ones who offer the most resistance to the help. This concept can be easily understood by observing it in the natural. A person who goes to the doctor for a regular check up concerning a common cold, will have a drastically different experience than the person who needs bones reset. For a common cold the doctor may say, "Let me listen to your chest" and ask the patient to take deep breaths. This patient will usually comply with little to no resistance.

Another patient, possibly involved in a freak accident, needs bones reset to save limbs, and to ensure that everything heals properly. Their injury is more severe, as is the treatment. To set their broken bones, this patient may need to be restrained by several strong men. The process is painful, but it's necessary. So it is in the spirit. I had to absorb this concept to keep from internalizing the disappointment of not being able to help some people.

The third and most poignant realization was most revelatory. I would be dismayed by the lackluster manner with which some approached ministry. I became regularly disappointed in some, because their full potential was not being realized. This disappointment stemmed from comparing how I served my former pastor with how others served under my leadership. It wasn't until the Lord revealed to me the reason for our differing approaches that I made amends with this.

As complicated as it seemed to me, the answer was actually very simple. I learned to understand them by becoming aware of how they view me. Some only view me as good entertainment, so nothing that I do or say is considered substantive to them. Some only view me as a good preacher. For these people, although they may enjoy my sermons, I have little to no ability to correct their wrongs, nor develop their character. Some only view me as their pastor. Thankfully, that relationship is all that is biblically required.

It was vitally important for a young pastor like myself to understand that it's okay that different people will see me differently. Eventually, I realized the important difference was that people could only respond to me based upon how they viewed me. As I compare my approach to servanthood and subordinate leadership to the approach of those who served under my covering, I learned something. Although I did view my pastor as a good preacher, I also accepted him as a good pastor. Most importantly, I embraced him not just as a pastor, not just as a preacher, but as a father.

Fathers pull a level of excellence out of their children that no one else can, whether those children be spiritual or natural. I realized that some people I will only be able to preach to, others I'll have the benefit of pastoring, and for a few, I'll have the privilege of fathering. It was important for me to understand that whatever relationship develops between me and those that I'm called to serve, as long as the Lord is pleased, I am at peace with it. I will not be everything to everybody, but I will be everything they allow me to be, by the help of God.

CHAPTER 15:

I LEARNED TO LEAN ON GOD, MY HEAVENLY FATHER

Psalms 27:10 reads "When my father and my mother forsake me, then the Lord will take me up." I vividly remember thinking, when I first arrived at the church that would serve as my spiritual training ground, "My life will change forever." If we're being honest, most of us would admit that our difficult moments proved to be our most dedicated teachers.

I acknowledge the trauma some elements of my spiritual upbringing caused. Likewise, I acknowledge and walk in all of the redeemable qualities that were instilled in me there. One of the greatest principles that undergirded

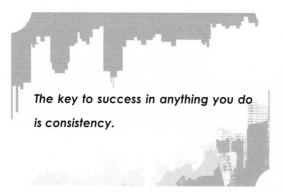

The key to success in anything you do is consistency.

my growth was consistency! Consistency was not only expected of me, it was demanded at all costs! That was okay, because I developed a mantra: *the key to success in anything you do is consistency.* That standard expectation ushered me into the maturity that I now possess. The day I learned that that expectation was real would have been for some the day they decided to never return.

I committed my life to Christ, and began my new journey to freedom. For some reason, I don't even remember why, I missed the following Bible study. At the very next service I attended, I got word that the pastor wanted to speak to me. Casually, I made my way to the front of the sanctuary. "Yes sir, you need to speak to me?" I asked. He responded swiftly, "Do you want to be saved or not?" Completely taken aback, I indecisively answered "Yes, sir." He then said, "Then you need to act like it! Considering the state you're in, you can't afford to miss any services!" At that moment, I had my first reality check.

I've told this story before, only to receive mixed reviews. Some people could appreciate the extreme expectation, believing that it was necessary for me. Others felt that this strict approach was unreasonable, and would prove to be a stumbling block for some new converts. Both could easily be true, depending on the person. However, for me, extreme expectations for high standards of behavior were necessary to help shape me into the man and Minister I would become. The discipline it produced in me bled over into every area of my walk. It impacted the way I measured the quality of my own effort.

As a result, I am a hard self critic, and I work hard at giving my absolute best effort! I took this mentality into my prayer life, and applied this dedication to my personal devotions. It was my former pastor who instilled in me the importance of prayer, fasting, and behavioral discipline. Most notably, he taught me the importance of living a prayerful lifestyle. Because of the deep void left by my fatherless past, I embraced him, not only as a pastor, but as the only father I knew. My desire to please him, and to be an honorable son, caused me to cling to the things he taught me.

I routinely practiced prayerfulness with intentionality. I began shutting in the church for days and sometimes weeks at a time. During my shut-ins, when I stayed in the church for extended periods of time, uninterrupted, I began to develop my own unique spiritual rituals. During the days and weeks that I was at the church, I would schedule time off work - so I wouldn't have to leave. I would often couple my prayer time with an extreme fasting regimen. In most cases, it would be what some call "absolute fasting" meaning no food and only water to drink.

During these times, I began to grow increasingly closer to God. Another notable by-product to these intimate times with God was that my loyalty to my spiritual father began to increase. I am forever indebted to that season of my life because at my lowest ministerial moments, I reverted to those behavioral disciplines and they're what ultimately got me through.

I remember, like it was yesterday, how often my former pastor told me both privately and publicly that I was not called to be a pastor. He began planting that seed long before I even considered pastoring. He openly declared on Sunday mornings, before the entire congregation, sometimes with no prompting and seemingly out of nowhere, "Elder Saucer is not a pastor. He can think he is but he is not a pastor!" Because of my loyalty to him and most importantly because I believed I could trust him, I never second-guessed him!

That's the primary reason why, when the Lord initially spoke to my heart concerning the call to Pastor, it shook me up and scared me to the point of disbelief. The sentiment and open declarations denouncing the possibility of God calling me to Pastor grew louder, and increasingly more aggressive, the closer I got to my departure. I now fully understand what was actually going on.

As a pastor of only a few years, I've gained access to the mind of God concerning his people in a way I've never experienced before. Without reservation, I can boldly say that part of a pastor's responsibility is to see into the future of the flock in order to guide them perfectly into the will of God for their life. If I could see the hidden potential in the people I serve after a few short years, I'm sure he could see what was in me before I could after 16-plus years. As much as it pains me to say this, he saw what was planted in me and instead of watering it, he tried to kill it!

My last Sunday there could accurately be described as a nightmare, depending on whose perspective it's viewed from. The sermon lasted more than an hour. Venom and esteem-killing serum pulsated through most of his words. He intended to break my heart and break my spirit. When the sermon concluded and the man I once revered as a father told my family and I to approach the altar, he proceeded to publicly pronounce a curse over us.

In one breath he said that my church would close in less than a year. With the next breath, he said our churches wouldn't fellowship until after a year has passed. With those two statements, he sent a strong message to me. He anticipated, and was rooting for my failure! That is still the most catastrophic moment, not just for my ministry, but for my entire life. However, it also proved to be a moment that defined me! I firmly believe that the way people respond to difficulty can be traced back to the way both God and life has hardwired them.

After my first spiritual father's public and destructive rejection, after I wiped my eyes and consoled my wife and family, the drive to succeed was ignited in my soul! The same words that were intended to bury me began to give me life! Knowing that there were people that I loved rooting for my failure became my greatest motivation. I closed my eyes that night and opened my eyes the next morning to a new-found dependency on God! The crutch I learned to lean on had been snatched from under me; I needed to learn to walk without him. My dependency on prayer, my commitment to my assignment, and the strength of my village got me to this point. People thought I would fail: that motivated me! People thought I was a walking curse: that motivated me! People thought their refusal to help me would cripple me: that motivated me! Ultimately, people thought I would quit; and that pushed me!

Today my testimony is of one who has been restored. When you fall out of one safe place, God will provide a place for you to land! I Corinthians 4:15 (KJV) declares, *"for though you have ten thousand instructors in Christ, yet have you not many fathers: for in Christ Jesus I have begotten you through the gospel."* One of the most discouraging parts about the loss of that relationship was the misconception that I could never have another relationship like it. I was grieved, believing that my one chance at being an honorable son was lost; but through divine intervention I became acquainted with a man who exemplifies what a pure manifestation of a father should be.

Initially, I was resistant to him because I was taught that you only have one spiritual father in your lifetime. This counterfeit vantage point caused my reluctance. As my current spiritual father continued to be consistently himself, I found myself searching the scriptures for answers. My research into what God had to say on the subject took me in many different directions, but I repeatedly ended up right back at the same phrase "you have not

You will not be fathered by many but you can be fathered by more than one!

many fathers". You will not be fathered by many but you can be fathered by more than one! A natural example of this comes from examining stepfathers, adoptive fathers and male caregivers. They may not be a biological father but that doesn't hinder them from actively fathering. I wrestled with this concept at the onset of my new father-son relationship. I wrestled until I lost! The truth is, a father's love will shine on you even when you seek shade. One father's rejection pushed me! Another father's love rescued me!

In closing, I've gained insight into fatherhood I never thought I'd have. My natural father prepared me to receive from my spiritual father, and my spiritual father prepared me to gain access to my Heavenly Father.

Now I am a dedicated natural father and now I am a committed spiritual father! Most of all, now I find vision, provision, safety, and identity in the arms of my Heavenly Father!

ABOUT THE AUTHOR

Elder Steve Saucer was born and raised in Dayton, Ohio. He attended Patterson Co-op High School and was a graduate of Colonel White High School. He was forced to overcome many challenges growing up in the inner city, but thanks to God's unseen protection coupled with Elder Saucer's will to succeed, he was able to endure and outlast the harshness of poverty.

After high school, Elder Saucer went on to serve his country in the United States Marine Corps. Shortly following his commitment to the United States Government, Elder Saucer was reintroduced to the matchless savior, Jesus Christ. The minister was baptized in Jesus' name under the oversight of the honorable Bishop Paul Bowers in Zanesville, Ohio. After receiving Christ as his personal savior he submitted himself to serving as a faithful member of a single church from 1999-2015. He preached his trial sermon in July of 2004 and was ordained an Elder in August of 2010. As a result of his faithful and unwavering commitment to God, the Lord has used him mightily in various areas of ministry. Elder Saucer served the church honorably in every capacity from usher to youth minister and as an Assistant Pastor for many years.

The first Sunday of November 2015 under the leading of the Holy Spirit according to the divine will of God, Elder Saucer was unctioned to establish Restoration Church! The Spirit spoke expressly to Pastor Saucer revealing to him that he had a unique ministry of Restoration and that it would be his life's mission to rebuild, restore and revive God's greatest creation... PEOPLE! Restoration Church experienced supernatural growth and favor. Growing a membership of more than 50 members in less than three months, and more than 100 in less than eight months. Restoration Church has experienced divine healing, detailed prophecy, holistic revival and so much more, all by the hand of God through the ministry of Pastor and First Lady Saucer!

Restoration Church of Jesus Christ is a proud P.C.A.F. (Pentecostal Churches of the Apostolic Faith) congregation. Pastor Saucer (and all subsequent ministries) is subject and submitted to the oversight and authority of the Honorable Bishop Lambert W. Gates, Sr., his pastor and spiritual father.

Pastor Saucer has ministered both nationally and internationally as an anointed evangelist. The Evangelist made a name for himself because of his selfless mentality and the supernatural signs and wonders that followed his ministry! He has ministered in prisons, nursing homes, street corners, boardrooms and many churches. Pastor Saucer has effectively crossed denominational, cultural and traditional barriers. Many have been saved, delivered, baptized in Jesus' name and filled with the precious gift of the Holy Ghost!

Aside from the spiritual servitude the Pastor exemplifies,

he is arguably most known for his tireless efforts outside of the walls of the church. Pastor Saucer is very community driven and has impacted the lives of people beyond explanation, some whom he may never get to meet. Pastor proudly serves as the Co-Chair on the Faith Based Advisory Committee for the Gem City Market. The Pastor is the visionary of an organic grow program that will feed and sustain countless Daytonians. He is the founder of Restore Life People Development Group, a 501c3 organization with the mission to "Restore Life to the Community by Developing the People in it." Which includes many programs such as: childcare, after school & literacy programs, aid for single mothers and helping the formerly imprisoned reacclimate to society. Pastor Saucer is affectionately referred to as "The People's Pastor."

Pastor Steve Saucer is the husband to Lawrensa Saucer, the father of three beautiful daughters and one handsome son. The minister is also the founder of Steve Saucer Ministries, where the mission is: Minister To The Needs of People! St. John 3:17 declares, "For God sent not His son into the world to condemn the world; but that the world through Him might be saved"! This verse embodies the spirit in which the pastor approaches his commission.

Pastor Steve Saucer's heart's desire is to win lost souls and strengthen the body of Christ through the preaching of the true and uncompromised Word of God!

THE FATHERLESS SON

Made in United States
North Haven, CT
04 July 2023

38545498R00074